"I finished my reading of this book more aware that God *is* wonderfully helpful in ways that matter; that he *is* faithfully reliable, always committed to doing me good; and that he *is* unfailingly involved, leading me in his sometimes inscrutable fashion toward everything I was created to enjoy."

From the foreword by **Dr. Larry Crabb**,
author of *A Different Kind of Happiness*

"Peace is a lot to expect from reading a book. But I've read this book cover to cover. It's here—a livable, biblical path laid out in a single verse that Jamie Rasmussen masterfully shows can help us settle for nothing less than genuine peace and joy. Let an outstanding pastor/theologian/leader point out a new way of thinking, which I needed to see and can change how you view and enjoy life as well. It is an 'I get this!' way of living and loving like Jesus that our hearts are desperate for. Our families need to see it in us, and a broken world longs for us to reflect it to them. Read this book!"

John Trent, PhD, Gary Chapman Chair of Marriage
and Family Ministry and Therapy, Moody Theological
Seminary; president of StrongFamilies.com; author
of *The Blessing* and *The Language of Love*

"Jamie Rasmussen uses thoughtful word studies and practical, real-life examples as he unpacks the meaning of eight seemingly abstract biblical words that the Bible uses to recalibrate our instinctive, habitual patterns of thought. Everyone who reads this book will be challenged to think in more God-centered, Christlike, Spirit-empowered ways!"

Wayne Grudem, PhD, research professor of theology and
biblical studies, Phoenix Seminary, Scottsdale, AZ

"I can't possibly read all the good Christian books that are published each year, but I do my best to read the great ones. This is one of them. It's great because it's a game changer. If you'd like internal joy to play more of a defining role in your daily life, Rasmussen's book shows you how to make that happen."

Dr. Tim Kimmel, author of *Grace Based Parenting* and *Grace Filled Marriage*

"For all the advice we have gotten about how to have a joyful life, Jamie has finally gotten to the core of the issue. True joy emerges not from our emotions or even our circumstances but rather from how we think! And given the fact that we can't control our emotions or our circumstances, realizing that we can control how we think is the first liberating step toward living joyfully. So what do you think? Follow Jamie's advice as he leads you on a thoughtful journey toward upbeat perspectives that bear the fruit of joy."

Dr. Joe Stowell, president of Cornerstone University, Grand Rapids, MI

"First, let me begin by saying I have known some very joyful people in the decades of my Christian experience—but none quite like Jamie Rasmussen! His very countenance is the embodiment of joy, and the words flowing from his heart in this volume have been beaten out on the anvil of personal experience. You will not be the same after reading and putting into practice the principles of this amazing and joy-filled book. Read it and reap!"

Dr. O. S. Hawkins, president and CEO of GuideStone Financial Resources; author of the bestselling Code series

"Amid the clamor and noise of creeping secular psychology, *How Joyful People Think* is boldly and biblically refreshing! It is not philosophy; it is the promise of God to those who live his principles and indeed are joy filled. Jamie Rasmussen takes a deep dive into the patterns of our living that will change how others view us and thus our Lord. An important read."

Naomi Rhode, CPAE Speaker Hall of Fame; cofounder of SmartPractice

"This book will guide you toward experiencing one of God's most profound promises—God's presence brings a joy that is even beyond his blessings."

Bill Thrall, mentor, Trueface Ministries

"Jamie Rasmussen draws on his extensive pastoral experience and deep meditation on Philippians 4:8 to encourage us to think the way God wants us to think. In a world in which our values and thinking patterns are often wrongly defined, this book challenges us to focus on God and the things he commends. It's not only the right thing to do but is also the sure path to God's blessing. I found this book very encouraging. It contains insights I want to tell others about."

Dr. Peter J. Williams, principal of Tyndale House, Cambridge

"So often in the Christian life, it is easy to let earthly trials rob us of the joy that is found in Christ. In *How Joyful People Think*, Jamie Rasmussen reminds us that the purpose of the Christian life is not to avoid or overcome suffering so as to reach temporal happiness but to unite ourselves with Christ in his suffering and glory. By doing so, Jamie provides a blueprint for how we can have a robustly Christian internal life that presents a cohesive witness to the world."

Alan Sears, founder of Alliance Defending Freedom

"Reading Jamie Rasmussen's book *How Joyful People Think* is a shot of joy itself, alongside a good dose of salty wisdom. Do you ever struggle with your temper? Your self-control? Your self-pity? In other words, are you human? Then read this book for a humorous, self-effacing, and biblically insightful battle plan. The Bible tells us that 'the way of the righteous is like the first gleam of dawn' (Prov. 4:18). This book shows you the way."

Greg Pritchard, PhD, director of European Leadership Forum; president of Forum of Christian Leaders

HOW
JOYFUL
PEOPLE
THINK

HOW
JOYFUL
PEOPLE
THINK

8 WAYS OF THINKING
THAT LEAD TO A BETTER LIFE

JAMIE RASMUSSEN

BakerBooks

a division of Baker Publishing Group
Grand Rapids, Michigan

Published by Baker Books
a division of Baker Publishing Group
PO Box 6287, Grand Rapids, MI 49516-6287
www.bakerbooks.com

Printed in the United States of America

Library of Congress Cataloging-in-Publication Data
Names: Rasmussen, Jamie, 1964– author.
Title: How joyful people think : 8 ways of thinking that lead to a better life / Jamie Rasmussen.
Description: Grand Rapids : Baker Publishing Group, 2018.
Identifiers: LCCN 2017059992 | ISBN 9780801075759 (pbk.)
Subjects: LCSH: Thought and thinking—Religious aspects—Christianity.
Classification: LCC BV4598.4 .R37 2018 | DDC 248.4—dc23
LC record available at https://lccn.loc.gov/2017059992

Unless otherwise indicated, Scripture quotations are from The Holy Bible, English Standard Version® (ESV®), copyright © 2001 by Crossway, a publishing ministry of Good News Publishers. Used by permission. All rights reserved. ESV Text Edition: 2011

Scripture quotations labeled KJV are from the King James Version of the Bible.

Scripture quotations labeled Message are from THE MESSAGE. Copyright © by Eugene H. Peterson 1993, 1994, 1995, 1996, 2000, 2001, 2002. Used by permission of NavPress. All rights reserved. Represented by Tyndale House Publishers, Inc.

Scripture quotations labeled NASB are from the New American Standard Bible®, copyright © 1960, 1962, 1963, 1968, 1971, 1972, 1973, 1975, 1977, 1995 by The Lockman Foundation. Used by permission. (www.Lockman.org)

Scripture quotations labeled NIV are from the Holy Bible, New International Version®. NIV®. Copyright © 1973, 1978, 1984, 2011 by Biblica, Inc.™ Used by permission of Zondervan. All rights reserved worldwide. www.zondervan.com

Scripture quotations labeled NLT are from the Holy Bible, New Living Translation, copyright © 1996, 2004, 2015 by Tyndale House Foundation. Used by permission of Tyndale House Publishers, Inc., Carol Stream, Illinois 60188. All rights reserved.

Scripture quotations labeled NRSV are from the New Revised Standard Version of the Bible, copyright © 1989, by the Division of Christian Education of the National Council of the Churches of Christ in the United States of America. Used by permission. All rights reserved.

18   19   20   21   22   23   24   7   6   5   4   3   2   1

green
press
INITIATIVE

To Kim

You are the most naturally joyful person I have ever found.
I am so blessed to have you as my wife.
Thanks for showing me how to choose joy.

CONTENTS

Foreword by Dr. Larry Crabb   13

Acknowledgments   17

Introduction   19

1. The Power of a Biblical "Whatever"   25
   Eight Ways of Thinking That Will Help You Get the Most Out of Life

2. Two Ways of Seeing   35
   Merging Personal Truth with Transcendent Truth
   "Whatever is true . . ."

3. Calm, Cool, Collected   53
   Embracing Wisdom in a World Gone Mad
   "Whatever is honorable . . ."

4. Thoughts That Heal   71
   Standing for True Justice
   "Whatever is just . . ."

11

5. The Myth of Individual Holiness   87
A Relational Approach to Purity
"Whatever is pure . . ."

6. Christian Hedonists   103
Why You Should Pursue Pleasure
"Whatever is lovely . . ."

7. Your Life on a Billboard   121
Where Who You Are Meets What Others See
"Whatever is commendable . . ."

8. A New Kind of Awesome   137
Linking Excellence to the Things That Matter
"If there is any excellence . . ."

9. Your Ace in the Hole   151
The Twin Tunnels of Praise
"If there is anything worthy of praise . . ."

10. A Peace-Driven Life   167
Getting the Most Out of Your Thinking
"Think about these things . . . and the God of peace will be with you."

Afterword   177

Notes   181

FOREWORD

I've been at this for more than fifty years, "this" defined as the effort to understand enough about the Christian life to actually *want* to live it, no matter the cost. The book you're about to read strengthened my belief that whatever the cost, it's worth it.

Over the six decades of my identity as a follower of Christ, I've found his words off-putting. In Luke 14:25–33, I hear Jesus saying something like this: "You want to be my disciple? Then count the cost. You must value relationship with me more than you value relationship with anyone else. And you must deny your appetite for immediate relief from the difficulties of life. And one more thing: you must not claim title to anything you own."

As both a somewhat reasonable and rational thinker (a source of pride) and an always thirsty soul eager for complete satisfaction now (a source of frustration), I once turned my back on Jesus. When I entered graduate school at age twenty, I kept my Christ-won ticket to heaven when I died in case the Christian thing turned out to be true. But I looked to self-help through psychology to enjoy the life I wanted to live before I got there. But five years of graduate study in clinical psychology left me desperate. The answers I was searching for simply weren't there. I came back to Jesus, chastened a bit but with a sulking spirit.

I still found God

unhelpful: I had problems he didn't solve;

unreliable: unanswered prayers outnumbered answered ones; and

uninvolved: I couldn't feel his presence with the same pleasurable intensity I experienced with my wife of then four years and a few close friends.

Now, five decades later, I still find God unhelpful, unreliable, and uninvolved. I still live with unsolved problems God could fix but doesn't. I still live with fervently expressed prayers that remain unanswered. And I still long to experience God's reality with consuming intensity more often than I do. But now in my seventies, the cross of Christ anchors my confidence in his goodness now and forever. Turning my back on the One who died for me is unthinkable.

But—there's always a "but"—more than ever I long to grasp whatever wisdom is needed to live well now, to benefit from biblical truth in a manner that empowers me to know joy in the midst of heartbreak, to know peace in the midst of life's storms, and to know what it is to love another when I'm feeling unsettled. *How Joyful People Think* provides much of the wisdom I need.

For several decades, Jamie Rasmussen and I have traveled through life together, exposing to each other our innermost struggles and encouraging each other with gospel hope. Jamie effectively and powerfully pastors a megachurch, but his identity is not a megachurch pastor. He is a pastor of people, a man who seizes his opportunities to lead, teach, and shepherd fellow followers of Jesus and to share good news with those not yet Jesus followers.

I just finished reading this book, slowly and thoughtfully, during a long plane ride. The hours passed quickly, a rare experience when cramped in coach for too much time. Three words came to mind as I read: precise, practical, and passionate.

Jamie settles for nothing less than careful, scholarly study of whatever passage is under consideration. Eight words recorded in Philippians 4:8 come alive in *precise* understanding of their meaning. The *practical* implications of what it would mean to live the wisdom of these eight words are clearly brought out. And thanks to Jamie's sensitive awareness of both his desire and his struggle to practice what he preaches, the *passionate* heart of a true pastor can be felt in every chapter.

I finished my reading of this book more aware that God *is* wonderfully helpful in ways that matter; that he *is* faithfully reliable, always committed to doing me good; and that he *is* unfailingly involved, leading me in his sometimes inscrutable fashion toward everything I was created to enjoy.

My part is to "think right," to think the way God wants me to think, to think the way that will bring joy, deliver peace, and release me to love, no matter what is happening in my life. This book makes clear what it means to "think right."

After reading Jamie's words, I find myself thinking right more than before, more aligned with God's way of thinking. *How Joyful People Think*, thoughtfully read, can do the same for you. My friend's book is a clear commentary on Paul's words in Romans 12:2: "Let God transform you into a new person by changing the way you think" (NLT).

Dr. Larry Crabb

ACKNOWLEDGMENTS

No book is written in a vacuum. Influences abound. The original ideas for this book were heard in oral form by the people of Scottsdale Bible Church in Scottsdale, Arizona. I can't thank them enough for their graciousness, love, and faith. Many of them have joy because they have learned to think along the lines of God's Word. A special thanks to the elders of Scottsdale Bible, under the leadership of Jeff Goble, who granted me a generous sabbatical leave in order to complete this project.

The early chapters were read closely by Larry Crabb, Tim Kimmel, Naomi Rhode, and my parents, Frank and Carolyn Rasmussen. It was their initial encouragement to keep writing that led me to continue to completion. A very special thanks goes to my wife, Kim, and my adult children, Hannah, Abby, and Paul, who allowed me time and space to write.

Chad Allen from Baker Publishing has been invaluable. He believed in this project very early on and provided direction and guidance from start to finish. The teams at Baker have been a joy to work with.

Bryan McAnally gets special credit for his help with a couple of the middle chapters. His skills in writing and editing were immensely helpful. My executive assistant, Kathy Mersbach, provided administrative and editing support, without which this book would never have been finished. Nick Palomo and Derek Brandt added creative ideas early on that helped me form and shape the direction of this book. Sonia Cleverly and Karen Saroian were amazing in providing final editing.

Last but not least: Tom Shrader kept me joyful and smiling while writing, Steve Uhlmann and Tyler Johnson consistently challenged my thinking, Darryl DelHousaye always had my back, and Kory Schuknecht asked every week how it was going. It's good to be in harness with people like these.

INTRODUCTION

Two psychologists from Cornell University conducted a fascinating study a few years back. They wanted to understand the role that *perspective* has in light of one's particular *circumstances*. To accomplish this, they studied Olympic medal winners, specifically the contrasting levels of satisfaction and happiness among gold, silver, and bronze winners. Measuring the athlete's facial expressions and body language immediately following their performance as well as while receiving their medal, these psychologists used a scale of 1 to 10 to determine the athlete's "happiness" response (1 being agony and 10 being ecstatic).

The results were surprising, and the data was overwhelming. The third-place bronze-medal winners were hands down quantifiably happier than the second-place silver-medal winners. Analyzing video footage of the 1992 summer Olympics in Spain, the psychologists found that immediately following the athletic competition and realizing the outcome, silver medalists scored an average of 4.8 on the happiness scale and bronze medalists an average of 7.1. The researchers observed similar responses when these same athletes subsequently received their medals during the awards ceremony.[1]

What conclusions did they draw? First and most obvious, third-place competitors were thrilled simply to have received a medal. They could have been a footnote to the event; instead, they got to stand on one of the three steps at the end. The second-place finishers, however, focused solely on how close they came to being first. This difference in perspective framed their thinking and was the determining factor in the level of happiness they experienced. The psychologists performing this study would go on to call this phenomenon "counterfactual thinking": the ability to think differently about a circumstance than the facts would appear to dictate. Or put even more plainly: the ability to have our thoughts make all the difference to our joy.

Our Thinking Matters

I think there is something to all of this. Some people go through a nasty marital breakdown and remain bitter the rest of their lives, while others who experience a similar breakdown become more loving, compassionate, and forgiving. Some people experience a childhood rife with economic struggles and become miserly for the rest of their lives, while others experience the same and become grateful and generous with their current financial blessings. Some people respond to vocational disappointment (whether it is having to work in a job they hate or losing a job they love) by becoming perpetually grumpy and moody, while others in the same scenario rise above it and find joy.

Why the difference? What is it that some people know or even do that others don't? How can some folks get a third-place medal and be happy, while others who compete in the same competition, perform better, and win a silver medal are much less happy? I submit that it all boils down to perspective—the ability to have our thoughts make all the difference to our joy.

This book is all about developing the right kind of thinking.

Beyond Positive Thinking

We must be careful at this point. Our culture already talks regularly and plentifully about "right thinking." The world has no shortage of self-help books, talk shows, leadership seminars, and church sermons that pine away about the virtues of the kind of thought life that leads to a fulfilling life. So why another book?

Here's why: when contemporary wisdom finds its voice on this subject, it usually weighs in with mantras that follow three trajectories: think positive, think possibilities, and think problem solving. These, contemporary wisdom insists, bring success in life, whether it be in our jobs, our relationships, our health, or even the spiritual realm. We are told that this threefold pattern of thinking determines our access to the good life. The more positive and possibility oriented our perspectives are, coupled with the ability to problem solve, the better life will be.

But, we must ask, to what end? If the goal is simply to nudge our emotions more toward the flowery end of the visceral spectrum, then thinking positive will often work. If the goal is to attain a higher level of achievement in our endeavors, then thinking possibilities will help. And if the goal is to get over the myriad hurdles that life presents, then having a problem-solving attitude will many times do the trick. Though there is certainly nothing wrong with these goals, I believe God wants more for us. He certainly wants something different than what we might be inclined to settle for. He doesn't want these kinds of temporal goals, which require only temporal thinking, for us.

God is much more concerned with a particularly different *kind* of thinking, which leads to a particularly different set of goals and results. This different kind of thinking involves altered perspectives and a more rigorous application than merely focusing on positives, possibilities, or problem solving. It requires learning to think in ways that God has clearly prescribed. It involves *learning to think as God wants us to think*. It's also the kind of thinking that will make us more mature in our personhood, more faithful to him, more loving toward others, and more satisfied within. It's the kind of thinking befitting a follower of Jesus Christ.

The famous Westminster Confession states, "Man's chief end is to glorify God, and to enjoy him forever." Glory and joy are what God is after: his glory and our joy. Thinking positive, thinking possibilities, and thinking problem solving are fine lines of thought when couched within our success-driven, security-oriented, quick-fix twenty-first-century culture, but they are not enough to deliver transcendent glory and eternal joy. There has to be more to God's economy, and thankfully, there is. God offers a way for us to experience counterfactual thinking in our own lives, but we must learn to live life from the vantage point of his declared mindset. Doing so involves his prescribed way of thinking.

In other words, don't settle. There is more. There is better.

God's Way of Thinking

This book is almost entirely concerned with one verse from the Bible—one rather long sentence tucked away within the concluding words of the New Testament book of Philippians. At first glance, the verse almost seems an afterthought, like some well-chosen parting words. However, if we allow ourselves to park in front of it, we soon realize that if any verse in the Bible is loaded with perspective-shaping truth, this is it. Though the Bible has many passages that reveal the kind of thinking God wants his people to embrace, this passage stands alone in its concentrated emphasis on God's way of thinking. It is jam-packed with profundity and richness, so much so that we could devote an entire book to it!

This verse comprises about three dozen well-chosen words, one of which is repeated six times. It asks us to consider no less than eight ways of thinking befitting people who desire to find their sufficiency and satisfaction in God. It's for people who want to learn to think differently—who don't want to settle for the status quo of current culture. These are God's attitudes for his people, and they are his way of allowing us to have regular counterfactual experiences as we make our way through all the ups and downs of life in this fallen world.

Here's the verse:

Finally, brothers, whatever is true, whatever is honorable, whatever is just, whatever is pure, whatever is lovely, whatever is commendable, if there is any excellence, if there is anything worthy of praise, think about these things. (Phil. 4:8)

Notice that each area of thinking is described using one word or a short phrase. Going back hundreds of years within combined Jewish and Greco-Roman cultures, each word and/or phrase is pregnant with meaning and loaded with application. We will spend some time with each word, and together we will get to know them as we would get to know a small group of good friends. And as we do with good friends, we will invite them into the living room of our minds and hearts and allow them to speak to us. Hopefully, we will allow them to change us from the inside out.

In fact, these words come with a promise. The very next verse says, "And the God of peace will be with you" (v. 9). God's way of giving us peace—real peace—is through our having the right kind of perspective. A perspective that allows us to trust him. A perspective that makes us want to follow him. Don't miss this: the perspective that God offers is also a perspective that helps us think as he wants us to think. The promise is that if you and I can learn to live life in light of these eight ways of thinking, "the God of peace" will share some of that peace with us.

To start our time with this verse, we'll look into God's way of thinking by focusing on a crucial mindset that forms a prerequisite for our journey into the eight ways of thinking. Then we'll explore each way of thinking in detail and what is involved in learning to think God's way.

1

THE POWER OF A BIBLICAL "WHATEVER"

Eight Ways of Thinking That Will Help You Get the Most Out of Life

I like good strong words that mean something.

Louisa May Alcott

When I was a boy growing up in the Midwest in the 1960s and 1970s, like many of us I was living in a culture in which words and their meanings were changing right before me. If something was originally described as "cool," it had a lower temperature measured in Fahrenheit or Celsius; then hippies redefined cool to describe people, places, and things that were attractive or inviting or agreed with their way of thinking. "Chick" originally meant a baby bird, but then it changed to mean a nice-looking girl (and some found this rather derogatory). "Smooth" first described the texture of an object, but then it morphed into describing how a person comes across to others.

Words change over time. Some words that become culturally entrenched in one generation get hijacked by the next generation and take on an entirely different meaning. It's sometimes hard to keep up with the changing meaning of some words, especially as we get older.

"Whatever"

Philippians 4:8 uses the same qualifying word for each line of thinking: *whatever*. It is repeated six times as a front-runner to each of the first six attitudes: whatever is true, whatever is honorable, whatever is just, and so on. Some scholars argue the repetition is poetic. Others argue it's for emphasis. My guess is both are true. What matters more is what *the author* meant by the use of this relatively common word.

Words change in their meaning. The meaning of this word has changed even within our own culture. In our day, the word *whatever* carries two vastly different definitions, reflecting a tension between a traditional meaning and a more contemporary one. Let's call them the "Doris Day" meaning and the "sarcastic teenager" meaning. In 1956, Doris Day sang "Que Sera, Sera" (Whatever Will Be, Will Be) in the Alfred Hitchcock thriller *The Man Who Knew Too Much*. The song quickly climbed the charts and became number two on the Billboard Hot 100. It won an Academy Award for best original song in 1956 and was the theme song for the *Doris Day Show* for five years running. It eventually made it onto the American Film Institute's list of the top one hundred songs in American cinema. The chorus of the song goes like this:

"Que sera, sera, whatever will be, will be. The future's not ours to see, que sera, sera. What will be, will be."

Mixing Spanish with English, this song uses the word *whatever* in a way that defined the mindset of a couple of generations. It is a song about accepting whatever comes. You can't control the future, so don't worry about it; just sit back and go along for the ride. Ultimately, "Que Sera, Sera" is a song about fate. Whatever happens will happen. In a time following the atrocities of two world wars and the Great Depression and with the global threat of communism, if there was one thing people in the mid-1950s knew, it was that you couldn't predict (let alone control) what was going to happen. "Whatever will be, will be."

With their carefree attitude, members of the counterculture movement of the 1960s took this concept even further, shunning societal norms in lieu of free love while traveling across the country in VW buses. "Whatever will be, will be." Though opposed to the biblical perspective, in which a sovereign God is in control of everything and is worthy to be trusted, the "Doris Day" meaning of the word became deeply ingrained in the psyche of Americans—many of whom still embrace this use of the word today.

But words and their meanings change. Though many people still use the word *whatever* in the traditional sense, a younger generation now uses it very differently. I affectionately call this the "sarcastic teenager" use of the word. We've all heard it used this way. You ask your teenager to clean up a mess, and the look you get is as if you just asked them to fly to the moon and plant a flag. You then repeat your request, this time with a little more authority behind it, and your teenager responds with the often-heard phrase

"Uh, like, whatever." It's clearly a dismissive, sarcastic, I-think-you're-an-idiot use of the word. Subtly different in tone, vastly different in meaning from the fate-laden "Doris Day" understanding, *whatever* is used by today's teenagers to communicate disagreement and a resigned acceptance. For them, saying "whatever" is a conversation stopper. They clearly mean, "I think you're wrong, but I know we won't see eye to eye on this. So let's move on."

To be fair, saying "whatever" could also be part of your teen's way of asserting their independence and separation from their family of origin. This is what adolescence is about. Still, it's just no fun being a parent on the receiving end of this dismissiveness.

Game Changer

Why is all this important? Why trace the meaning over the last sixty years of a common word from its "whatever will be, will be" use to its current "like, whatever" use? Here's why: neither of our contemporary uses of the word *whatever* comes anywhere close to what Philippians 4:8 means by this word. If the use of a word can change within a generation or two, imagine how it can change in two thousand years over many generations and across different cultures.

When the apostle Paul, inspired by God, originally wrote Philippians 4:8, the word *whatever*, repeated six times, was a common one in the Greco-Roman culture of the first century. It is the Greek word *hosos* (pronounced *HAH-sahs*), and the New Testament writers used it some 115 times. The word also appears literally thousands of times in Greek literature from the ancient world. However, what is most fascinating about this word is that it is a positive word—even an inspirational word—primarily used to describe the *extent* of something. One prominent Greek-English lexicon defines *whatever* as "as much as; as long as."[1] It is a word used to refer to limitless volume and extent.

A rather pictorial example of this meaning emerges in the Gospel of John, where the writer used this word to describe the miracle of the feeding of five thousand people. He wrote, "Jesus then took the loaves, and when he had given thanks, he distributed them to those who were seated. So also the fish, *as much as* [*hosos*] they wanted" (John 6:11, emphasis added). The people ate "as much as [whatever]" their hearts desired. A couple of fish miraculously multiplied to feed five thousand. The word used is *hosos*—a visionary word used to expand the possibilities and broaden the horizons.

I believe Paul the apostle used this word the same way in Philippians 4:8. He prefaced each particular way of thinking with a resounding *whatever* to get us to dream about all the possibilities this kind of thinking can have when applied to our lives. He challenges us to approach each God-ordained perspective with a Spirit-led creativity and a vision that conjure in our mind's eye what these possibilities might look like as we learn to think along these lines. "Whatever is true, whatever is honorable, whatever is just . . . whatever . . . whatever . . . whatever." He invites us to dream big on a very personal level. Paul used the word *whatever* to show us how to turn a couple of fish into a full-course meal when it comes to how we think.

To see how potent the use of this somewhat commonplace word is in this verse, imagine how it would read if *whatever* was *not* included. The verse would say, "Finally, brothers, [if something] is true, honorable, just, pure, lovely, commendable, excellent, [and/or] worthy of praise, think about these things." Certainly, it doesn't become a bad verse; it is somewhat stoic and paternalistic maybe but still pretty good stuff.

However, like a scratched CD stuck on the same phrase, the repetition of the word *whatever* catches our attention. By repeatedly weaving this word throughout the verse, God makes his message clear: *whatever* is intended to be applied to each of the eight ways of thinking. We are led to envision much more within our thinking and to explore endless God-enabled possibilities. We are offered the opportunity to ponder all the implications and applications imaginable as we learn to think with God's perspective in mind. We can approach each moment of each day with a passion born of thousands of potentialities as we learn to think with truth, honor, purity, love, and excellence leading the way in our minds and hearts. No longer do we have to follow the pattern of our culture with a passive "whatever will be, will be" in mind. Nor do we have to go through each day with a sarcastic, dismissive "whatever" trailing behind us. We can now live with the power of a biblical whatever guiding us through each thought we have and each choice we make. It's a game changer if there ever was one.

Imagining the Possibilities

Let me show you how this might work. One of the things I tend to struggle with is frustration while driving. I wouldn't say I ever engage in road rage, but I can get frustrated in urban traffic, especially at the end of a long day or when I am in a hurry to get somewhere. By the time I finally arrive at my destination, my mood can really be spoiled. I'm not alone. A recent AAA national study of 2,705 licensed drivers found that nearly 80 percent of them reported "significant anger" while driving at least once in the past year. Even scarier, the report found that over half of the drivers surveyed admitted to tailgating an offending vehicle and that just under half of them admitted to yelling or honking their horn at another driver.[2]

This is where the power of a biblical whatever can become a game changer. Say somebody cuts me off in traffic or is going too slow in the fast lane (which should be one of the seven deadly sins). What I have practiced over the years is to slow down (literally and figuratively) and filter my thinking through the eight thought arenas of Philippians 4:8. I then apply the power of a biblical whatever to each one to determine the creative possibilities each might entail. Here is what this practice looks like in this situation:

"Whatever is true": Well, it is true that the person in front of me doesn't know how to drive as well as I do. Few people do. But it's also true that I sometimes do what they did. I cut people off now and then. I get caught holding someone up in the fast lane if I am not paying attention. I don't mean to, but if truth be known (as it is right now), I sometimes do these things too. I guess I'm more of a hypocrite than I want to admit. Maybe I should cut this guy some slack.

"Whatever is honorable": Though I am tempted to lash out and join the 50 percent of tailgaters, honkers, and yellers, I can't see God or even my wife seeing that as honorable. Honor would look differently than lashing out or responding rashly. Let's protect my honor and take the high road (pun intended).

"Whatever is just": It is probably just and fair that there should have been a cop present to see what this person did (where are they when you need them?). However, there wasn't. Justice wasn't served *again*. But it's not my role to take matters into my own hands. We have traffic officers and traffic cameras for such situations. It's my job to back off and get to where I am going safely—and with my integrity intact. And though it's hard to see justice skirted, the alternative is worse. So I'm moving on (literally).

"Whatever is pure": Purity is the ability to be good and relate well. This is how God demonstrates purity. There would be no purity in showing someone any of my fingers, save for my thumb pointing straight up! So if I do show any finger, that will be the one. Better yet, let's just move on. I have better places to be than here.

Before I know it, with just half of the thought arenas of Philippians 4:8 applied to the problem at hand, combined with the power and vision of a biblical whatever leading the way, I am already feeling better. In fact, just going through this mental exercise distracts me from what else I might have been thinking as it focuses my mind elsewhere (even upward). Joy is right around the corner.

The obvious point is that Philippians 4:8 provides new ways of thinking. The power of a biblical whatever ignites them with possibilities and vision. With a renewed perspective comes a renewed focus. And many times focus is what

32

God uses to help us see our way through a problem to the other side.

How many scenarios occur in your daily life that could use the power of a biblical whatever? Maybe it's

- a decision at work that has you perplexed;
- what to do with your teenager who each day is increasingly distant from you;
- a personal habit that continues to get the best of you, and you can't seem to see your way clear to victory; or
- a nagging spiritual problem such as doubt, confusion, discouragement, or fear.

I wonder what slowing down and filtering your thought process through the grid of the eight perspectives of Philippians 4:8 would teach you. The power of a biblical whatever is bound to make a difference.

With a firm grasp of the power of a biblical whatever driving each of the eight perspectives, we are now ready to begin exploring and discovering a new kind of thinking God has for his people. We are now ready to dive deep into the realities of Philippians 4:8. Unlike any kind of cognitive therapy our world offers today, this way of thinking promises to transform. How could it not? It comes from God.

Let the journey begin.

2

TWO WAYS OF SEEING

Merging Personal Truth with Transcendent Truth

"Whatever is true . . ."

A realist is an idealist who has gone through the fire and
been purified. A skeptic is an idealist who has gone through
the fire and been burned.

Warren Wiersbe

I have had the privilege of being a pastor for more than
twenty-five years. During this time, I have interacted with all
kinds of people in all kinds of settings. Here is one thing I
have noticed about humanity in general when it comes to our
overall attitude: some of us lean toward an overly *negative*
view of life and circumstances, while others lean toward an
overly *positive* view of the same life and circumstances. In

other words, very few of us go through our daily thoughts about known reality in a well-balanced way. We might think we do, but we really do not.

The best indicator of balanced or unbalanced thinking is how a person handles bad news. It is probably the most accurate gauge for measuring the focus and content of a person's thinking. Following are some examples of unbalanced thinking:

> "We saw something on the last mammogram [or if you are a man, PSA test] that concerns us, and we want to do a biopsy."
>
> > **Negative people:** "I knew it. I knew it was going to be bad. I could just feel it. My life is probably over. Here I come, Lord."
> >
> > **Positive people:** "There's simply no way that I could have cancer. God wouldn't allow it at this time. It's not possible. I know the biopsy will be negative. I'm going to receive good news."

> "We are announcing that our company is going to merge with another company, and some roles will be eliminated."
>
> > **Negative people:** "It's over. I better get my résumé updated. They certainly won't keep me. And forget about getting another job like this. I might as well put the house up for sale and turn in my car lease."
> >
> > **Positive people:** "There's no way they would ever let go of me. Why would they? They know what they've got. I've got nothing to worry about."

"This is Principal Evans calling. I want to talk to you about your son. We have some concerns."

Negative people: "What did he do now? I know this can't be good. Ever since he was three, this kid has been an accident waiting to happen. I guess it's time to face the music."

Positive people: "Why would you have concerns about my kid? He's a really good kid. He's a little messy maybe, and sometimes whimsical, but a darling child. What could he have done that is so bad?"

As the old saying goes, "There are essentially two kinds of people: people who see the glass as half full and those who see the glass as half empty." Which are you? We each tend to lean one way or the other.

That's the point. We *lean*. Few of us have a perspective that is 100 percent reality based. When it comes to our relationships, our circumstances, our view of current events, and even our view of God, the fall of humankind has affected our thinking. I know I have leaned toward a more negative, cynical side ever since I was a little guy. I'm not proud of that. It's how my fallen nature responds to life. I long for a better balance. I long for more reality.

"Whatever Is True"

The first biblical whatever of Philippians 4:8 challenges us to think about what is true. It's talking about reality—known reality—and challenging us to think and live in light of known reality.

The word translated "true" is *alethes* (pronounced *a-lay-THASE*) in the original Greek language in which Philippians was written. In its root form, it means "nonconcealment."[1] The idea is to disclose what really is, whether involving a body of knowledge or the truth behind a personal experience. The Greek philosopher Plato used this word to describe what he called "true and genuine" as opposed to what was only a "reflection and appearance" (i.e., only appearing to be true).[2] The New Testament authors used *alethes* twenty-five times, each time to refer to that which is true, real, and/or honest. *Alethes* is closely associated with knowledge and life in general.

What is most fascinating about the use of the word *alethes*, however, is that it can refer contextually to either transcendent truth or personal truth. And there is a huge difference.

Always and Everywhere

Transcendent truth is generally understood as truth unaffected by time and space. It is truth that is "out there" (always and everywhere), waiting to be discovered. It transcends us and hence is not dependent on our individual or communal lives (i.e., what we do or think) in order to be true. Transcendent truth is the kind of truth that is true whether or not we recognize it or believe it. It is true by the very nature of its transcendent reality.

For Christians, transcendent truths are grounded in the trinitarian God and his revelation to us, the Bible. These truths include the existence and reality of God, the goodness of God, the unchanging and sovereign nature of God, the fallenness of humankind, and the mercy and forgiveness of

God through Jesus. We rightly formulate these truths into firmly held doctrines about God and the nature of spiritual reality. These truths are transcendent in their very nature, for they are contained in God himself and thus are absolute and unchanging.

It's important for us to grasp this understanding of transcendent truth when it comes to how we think because *alethes* is used this way many times in the New Testament. For instance, at one point in Jesus's earthly ministry, some notable political and religious leaders made this comment to Jesus: "Teacher, we know that you are true [*alethes*] and teach the way of God truthfully [*aletheia*], and you do not care about anyone's opinion, for you are not swayed by appearances" (Matt. 22:16). These astute leaders clearly recognized Jesus's character and words as "true," in that they were tied to "the way of God" and not to anything earthly, such as others' opinions or vain reputation. They recognized that there was something transcendent about Jesus and the things he taught. Something otherworldly. Something bound up in God himself. Even something eternal.

Another example of the usage of *alethes* as transcendent truth is found in the words of Jesus himself: "Even if I do bear witness about myself, my testimony is true [*alethes*], for I know where I came from and where I am going" (John 8:14). Here, Jesus linked his teaching to his transcendent nature ("I know where I came from"), and this nature served as proof that his teaching was from God and was true. He said that his words were definitely and surely true precisely because they were eternal in nature (i.e., from where he came and to where he was going). His words—and the truth they expressed—were transcendent.

Other New Testament writers likewise used the word *alethes* to denote transcendent truth. Peter made it clear that his Spirit-infused writings were "the true [*alethes*] grace of God" (1 Pet. 5:12). John posited the same when he wrote about the command to love and argued that this command was made "true [*alethes*] in him [i.e., Jesus]" (1 John 2:8).

If we end our exploration of the word *alethes* simply by noting this particular aspect of its use in the New Testament, we will conclude that our thinking, as it relates to Philippians 4:8, is to be grounded in transcendent truth. What we think should focus on what is eternally true—the truth that comes from God and is taught in the Bible.

Here and Now

But not so fast. Our journey of tracing the use of *alethes* is not yet over. The New Testament writers used this same word to refer to a kind of truth that we will call personal truth. Personal truth is the truth of one's own experience. It is grounded not in the transcendent but in what philosophers call the immanent, the here and now. While transcendent truth is unaffected by time and space, personal truth is contained *within* time and space—your time and space. It is something that is true *for you*—and many times just for you, as it is grounded in your experiences and perceptions.

Though personal truth certainly may overlap with transcendent truth (we will get to this shortly), it doesn't have to do so in order to be true. For example, at one point in his public ministry on earth, Jesus interacted with a Samaritan woman at a local watering hole. While talking with her about her life, the following interchange took place:

40

The woman answered him, "I have no husband." Jesus said to her, "You are right in saying, 'I have no husband'; for you have had five husbands, and the one you now have is not your husband. What you have said is true [*alethes*]." (John 4:17–18)

Obviously, *alethes* was used differently here than in the previous examples. It referred to the fact that this woman had been married five times and was not married to the man she was currently living with. This was not a transcendent truth (unaffected by time and space); it was a highly personal truth (contained within this woman's time and space and personal to her). The truth surrounding this woman's marital history was not "above and beyond" us, somehow wrapped up in the personhood of almighty God. The truth of her multiple marriages was rather an intimately personal truth (true for her) that described the personal reality she was experiencing.

Luke used *alethes* in a similar way. When he described Peter's miraculous release from prison by an angel of God, he said, "And he [Peter] went out and followed him [the angel]. He did not know that what was being done by the angel was real [*alethes*, "true"], but thought he was seeing a vision" (Acts 12:9). Peter's experience of being led out of prison was real and true (it was grounded in known reality), even though he thought he might have been imagining it. Again, this is an example of *alethes* being used to describe a personal reality rather than a transcendent one.

Two Realities

Why trace the dual usage of the word *alethes* through its transcendent and personal contexts? Why is this significant?

What does it have to do with Philippians 4:8 and the way we are to think?

What we need to understand is this: all transcendent truth can and should become personal truth, but not everything we call personal truth is transcendent in nature or even real. This is an extremely important and helpful distinction to make. Much of our thinking can and should be about the *intersection* of our personal reality (our truth) with God's transcendent reality (God's truth) as outlined in his Word (the Bible) to us. At the same time, we must be careful to distinguish between the two and not to label all personal reality as transcendent reality for the simple reason that faulty perceptions and skewed logic are common among fallen human beings.

As we have seen, all transcendent truth by its very nature is true, for it is bound up within a transcendent reality that is above and beyond us. At the same time, this doesn't mean that all personal truth is real, as evidenced by the fact that Peter doubted his own perceptions when he was released from prison. Let's explore this rich biblical distinction further to discover a couple of thought-shaping implications.

First, when transcendent truth intersects with personal truth, we are grounded in "what is." As a pastor, I have the privilege of a front-row seat to these kinds of intersections on a regular basis. Not too long ago, following one of our Sunday morning worship services, a woman came up to me and shared some bad news she'd recently received about the status of her current employment. In a fragile economy and postrecession culture, she was facing the potential loss of her job. It was a good job, which she had held for a while, and it had provided well for her as a single parent with two young children. Finding similar work with a commensurate salary would be difficult.

What happened next in our conversation was both real and raw. She said, "Pastor, I know that God is both good and sovereign. I know that none of this surprises him and that he is in full control. I know that he is faithful to me and my kids. But I am still afraid. And this feels huge." Right before me, in what many would see as a rather common and almost daily emotional struggle, the personal was intersecting with the transcendent. This dear woman was in a battle for known reality. She was courageously recognizing her personal reality without becoming either overly positive or overly negative. Her personal situation was real and huge and scary. But she was also fighting hard within her mind and heart to cling to the transcendent truth of God's faithfulness, goodness, and providential care.

Because I have learned to appreciate the journey of faith and the process it takes, I simply prayed with and for her. I prayed that God would keep her right where he had her. I prayed that his power and presence would guide her into even deeper and richer waters of trust and assurance. I prayed that God would continue to provide in obvious and unmistakable ways for her and her children. In short, I wanted to help her stay in the intersecting realm of the personal and the transcendent, knowing that this was her best shot at peace.

The story has a happy ending. God answered our prayer for protection of this woman's job. He also gave her peace through the situation. I'm glad this friend of mine allowed herself to think about "whatever is true." I'm glad she did not shy away or run from the intersection of transcendent truth and personal truth.

There are plenty of moments in our daily lives when our personal reality bumps up against God's transcendent reality. On the one hand, this intersection might involve a problem at work, bad news about one of the kids, or a nagging family-of-origin issue that keeps rearing its ugly head. It might even involve a crisis of faith or doubt. On the other hand, this intersection might occur at the moment of an unexpected blessing, an unanticipated joy, or an experience of the beauty of nature.

The Great Centering

I call this intersection of personal and transcendent realities the "great centering." It is God's truth meeting our truth. It is what will keep us from becoming one of the overly negative or overly positive people we spoke of at the beginning of this chapter. Learning to recognize, focus on, and honor both transcendent reality and our own personal reality keeps us centered on the true nature of life in all its fullness—physically, emotionally, intellectually, relationally, and spiritually. Learning to think and live in light of what is true grounds us in what is, whether our circumstances are good or bad, up or down, exciting or mundane. Whenever our truth intersects with God's truth, we are firmly in the realm of known reality. And God is always found there.

This centering is precisely what happened to the five-time-married woman at the well. As her personal truth was uncovered and declared for what it was, complete with her marital breakdowns and current relationship with man number six, she experienced the intersection of her personal reality with transcendent reality in the very presence of the embodiment

44

of transcendent reality, Jesus himself. As she interacted with him within the honesty of her personal reality, she began to discover and experience new relational life as the personal intersected with the transcendent. She discovered that God is more real than she imagined. She realized that God wants to be worshiped "in spirit and truth" (John 4:23). She longed for what Jesus called "a spring of water welling up to eternal life" (v. 14). She even got to the point where she wondered, "Can this be the Christ?" (v. 29). Spiritual sparks flew as the personal interacted with the transcendent. She was learning to think in light of known reality. Her perspective concerning her circumstances was shifting. And her soul was being nourished. By the end of the story, the implication is that this woman came to grips with the reality of Jesus, even as many others within her Samaritan community recognized Jesus as "the Savior of the world" (v. 42).

In the moments of intersection of the personal and the transcendent, we experience what one of my longtime mentors called "God sightings." These are moments when we have the opportunity to "think reality." When these moments happen, we must recognize reality for what it is and allow our personal reality to fully intersect with transcendent reality. We must allow the transcendent truth of God, in whatever biblical form he presents it, to have its intended influence over our personal reality. Understanding our personal reality through the perspective of God's transcendent truth will truly ground us in what is, and God will meet us at this point. He will give us his peace and joy when we stay centered at this intersection.

Having discussed the grounding effect of seeing the personal in light of the transcendent, I now want to point to a second profound implication of seeing the distinction between these two realities: a healthy distinction between personal truth and transcendent truth keeps us open and humble in our daily attitudes.

A few years back I served on the board of directors for a wonderful and much-needed nonprofit agency. As can be common with these kinds of endeavors, we were having problems attaining unity at the board level. This particular organization had a wonderful fifty-year history of serving those in need. But in many organizations with long histories, people can get stuck in their ways and be less sharp. When this happens, both personnel and programs usually need to be changed. This is what we were up against, and our board was not unified. I've never been afraid to seek outside expertise, so at one point, as an officer of the board, I retained a wise, seasoned organizational consultant to spend a day with us and give us his input.

I will never forget what happened the day we were all together at a retreat center in Arizona. I shared with the other members that I didn't understand their resistance to my ideas for change and growth. I said, "I am very careful what proposals I bring to you as a board. In fact, I don't bring anything that I haven't thought about and worked on for months—sometimes years. So when I do bring ideas to you, I am 90 percent sure they are right and good for the future of our agency."

At this point, the consultant looked up and carefully asked, "Jamie, what would happen if you brought this board an idea that was 50 percent baked and then let them wrestle with the rest?" I wasn't prepared for that question. I had been operating as a community leader and following my method of preparation for almost twenty years by that point. I responded, "Well, that would be sloppy in my mind. Presenting ideas and proposals I haven't completely worked through first would present a vulnerability to my leadership. My dad was a lawyer, and this is how he prepared for big cases. The method served him well, and I'm just following suit."

Our wise consultant smiled at me and said, "But this isn't a court of law, and your fellow board members are not a jury. You are trying to find God's direction for this organization together, and you're trying to breed unity. You have more than a dozen seasoned board members here who respect each other and believe in the mission. Do it together and bring them your ideas sooner."

This was a watershed moment for me in my life and leadership. I realized I had been placing confidence in my own decision-making—and then trying my best to convince my fellow leaders that I was right. Since that time I have disciplined myself to include others early on in the formation process of my thinking. I have learned that my personal truth is not always as solid as it seems to me and that I need the power of multiple minds and hearts speaking into the circumstances of my life. This epiphany gave me fresh appreciation for the wisdom expressed in the Bible: "A cord of three strands is not quickly broken" (Eccles. 4:12 NIV) and "Without counsel plans fail, but with many advisers they succeed" (Prov. 15:22). It's probably no coincidence that the organization I was serving ended up making the right changes and to this day is increasing in size and effectiveness. Not unrelated, my wife thinks I am a better person to be around too.

Here's the point: if I hadn't drawn a distinction between my personal truth and God's unchanging, solid, transcendent truth, I would not have found the humility to consider that maybe my particular take on reality was flawed. I would not have been able to work well with those around me. Too often I tried to add transcendent weight to my personal truth, and doing so almost always got me in trouble.

You Are Not God

One of the reasons it is important to distinguish between God's transcendent truth and our personal truth is because doing so honors the fact that God's truth is always correct; this is not always the case with our truth. We all know this. It's just hard to admit it. Consider the following scenarios:

- We argue with our spouse or a good friend, and we are absolutely convinced we are right and they are wrong.
- Our boss makes a decision we disagree with, and we inwardly label them crazy.
- Our adult children parent in a certain way, and we wonder what happened to the good old days.
- Conversely, our parents tell us to do something, and we are convinced they have no idea what they are talking about or are out of touch with the times.

These are examples of personal realities we deal with on a regular basis. What complicates each situation is that many times we approach our personal reality as if it were transcendent in nature (as if the truth has come to us from on high). We give our personal reality the same weight as God's eternal truth. We might even try to find a Scripture verse or two to make our point and feel justified all the while. Then we wonder why we have so much relational friction with those around us.

Think what would happen if we recognized and truly honored the fact that *alethes* refers to both God's unchanging transcendent truth, which comes to us through his Word, and our personal truth, which is affected by our fallen nature. What might our lives look like if, in our perceptions, we gave the proper weight to each side? What might our lives look like if we were more conviction oriented about God's truth and more openhanded and humble about our truth? At the very least, doing so might make us more likable and easier to be around.

In the vein of a biblical whatever, let's dream of all the possibilities that surround our lives when we learn to "think reality." When we confront the good and the bad, let's contemplate the intersection of personal reality and transcendent reality with an honest look at our circumstances that doesn't flinch at God's promises. Let's give proper weight in our thinking to the distinction between personal truth and transcendent truth. "Whatever is true . . . think about these things."

Experiencing God

Let's go back to where we started. The medical test results need to be heard. The company merger is going through and downsizing will occur. The kid is in the principal's office and a meeting has been called. These are the personal realities we have to deal with. The glass-half-empty people say, "'Whatever is true, think about these things'? Well, these difficult situations right in front of me are true. And they stink. Life stinks. Nothing ever goes my way." The glass-half-full people say, "Look on the bright side. Here's what's true: at least I'm alive! I'm breathing. All is not lost. I can live to see another day (albeit possibly fighting cancer, jobless, and with a rebellious kid)."

Our culture's way of thinking about and responding to these kinds of situations offers us either soul-sucking pessimism or superficial optimism. There may be some helpful possibilities thrown in, such as "Find the best cancer treatment," "Send your résumé out and get networking," "Find the kid a good therapist," but they still leave many wondering, "Isn't there more? Isn't there a better perspective? Where is God in this? Where are the 'streams of living water' Jesus talked about?"

What if in our thinking we allowed the personal to intersect with the transcendent—we allowed our personal circumstances to intersect with God's transcendent reality based on his promises? God promises a rich sense of his *presence* during hard times (see Jesus's words in Matt. 18:20). He promises divine *purpose* in the middle of chaos (see Paul's experience in 2 Cor. 4:16–18). He even promises *power* when we need it most (see Paul's experience in 2 Cor. 12:7–10). Presence. Purpose. Power. Now we're getting somewhere. What if our very lives could intersect with those? They can. But we must think about "whatever is true." We must face God's transcendent truth in the midst of our personal reality. Here is how it works:

> The person facing the potential bad news from the doctor might think, "Yes, this could be bad. This could change

my life as I know it. But I don't know anything yet. I haven't even heard the results of the test. But God has. And God says that all my days were set for me before even one of them came to pass. So none of this surprises him. His presence is with me."

The person facing the potential job loss might think, "This is scary, unsettling to say the least. But I've had similar experiences in the past, and God always seemed to demonstrate some sort of purpose in and through them. I'll bet he is up to something now as well. I'm going to hang on for the ride!"

The person facing the meeting in the principal's office might think, "Most parents are not called to this office to let them know their kid is doing great. Maybe this is the exception, but probably not. I need strength for this one. And I know that God is in the business of giving us just enough strength when we need it to handle whatever comes our way. I choose to focus on this reality."

Presence, purpose, power: God's transcendent promises intersecting with our messed-up lives. Now that's a great way to think! And who knows, as C. S. Lewis once said, we just might end up being "surprised by joy."[3]

3

CALM, COOL, COLLECTED

Embracing Wisdom in a World Gone Mad

"Whatever is honorable . . ."

A big part of Christian maturity is learning to let God keep
you steady and to be ruled less and less by your emotions
and circumstances.

Twila Paris

Have you ever had an experience in which you risked sharing
something about yourself with another person—something
that would cause the majority of people to react with shock,
anger, or even repulsion—only to have the person you shared
it with not react that way? Has this ever happened to you?
My guess is it has.

Some people experience this when they see a professional
counselor. They share things that would cause an average

person to react strongly, but the counselor doesn't respond this way. And this is why they go back.

In a similar vein, my Catholic friends tell me they experience this in a confessional with a priest. They share things that would cause most of their friends to respond with shock or harsh judgment, but the priest doesn't. He responds with a listening ear and a tone and tenor of grace and forgiveness. And this is why they go back.

Others tell me this is what their closest friendships are like. They have the freedom to share their deepest and darkest stuff without fear of reprisal. Instead, they receive relational acceptance combined with cogent wisdom. And this is why they go back.

Jesus said, "Judge not, that you be not judged" (Matt. 7:1). Though most of us like the idea behind these words, we've been around the block enough times to know that it's rare to find a person who truly lives up to these words. And so we go through life with our guard up, not letting too many people (if any) get too close.

A Nonreactionary Spirit

There is something about a nonreactionary spirit that makes us feel welcome and safe. This spirit is marked by steadiness and grace. It comes across as thoughtful and wise. A person with this kind of spirit thinks deeply and richly before they act or respond. This is the type of relationality most of us are naturally drawn to and to which we desire to open up our lives.

I believe a nonreactionary spirit is what initially attracted people to Jesus when he walked this earth. For example, in

John 8, Jesus encountered a woman who had been caught in adultery and deeply shamed by the religious leaders. Jesus, however, didn't join in their shame game. He wasn't shocked or scandalized by her sin. Instead, he calmly drew in the dirt with his finger—a rather serene and contemplative act—and then uttered these famous words: "Let him who is without sin among you be the first to throw a stone at her" (v. 7).

Or how about when Peter, one of Jesus's closest followers, denied ever knowing Jesus? Peter felt shame all by himself. He didn't need the religious leaders' help on this one. Jesus responded with a threefold call to love (hardly reactionary and judgmental), which drew Peter back into the fold.

And the list goes on. Think of all the people with whom Jesus interacted: Matthew at the tax collector's booth; the unnamed woman who touched Jesus in the crowd in order to be healed; the paralytic who interrupted Jesus's teaching when his friends dropped him through the roof; vertically challenged Zacchaeus, who had to climb a tree to get a glimpse of Jesus. What these interactions have in common is a nonreactionary Jesus, a Jesus filled with grace and understanding mixed with life-giving passion and truth. These people encountered a calm, cool, and collected Jesus in their interactions with him.

The point for us is clear: maturing Christians learn to think in a nonreactionary way. They learn to view the world around them with the same calm, cool, and collected composure that Jesus demonstrated. This is the same mindset we are drawn to in those we feel the safest around. This is the same mindset that brings peace and joy.

"Whatever Is Honorable"

The next line of Philippians 4:8 challenges us to think about "whatever is honorable." This is an interesting, if not difficult, word in the original Greek of the New Testament. It's the word *semnos* (pronounced *sem-NAHS*), and it is used only four times in the New Testament. Its cousin *semnotes* (pronounced *sem-NAH-tace*) is used an additional three times. *Semnos* is rendered by most Bible translations as "noble, honorable, dignified."

This word was used by the ancient Greeks to describe the Greek gods (such as Zeus and Hermes). *Semnos* referred to their greatness and majesty. It was used to convey their loftiness and their deserving honor and worship. By the time it was picked up by the New Testament writers, however, the word had morphed into a term used to describe human beings who were marked by "seriousness" or "solemnity."[1] It carried with it the idea of gravity and weightiness, describing a person who was thoughtful and steady, a person not easily swayed by outward happenings.

Maybe it makes sense, then, that in the New Testament, this rarely selected word was used to describe what a deacon (and even a deacon's spouse) should be like (1 Tim. 3:8, 11). A deacon was a church leader who served others through tangible, helpful acts. A deacon also acted as a provider of wisdom in tough situations. We are first introduced to deacons in Acts 6, where they are found serving widows in need. They even mediated disputes between widows. The description given them is apt: "men of good repute, full of the Spirit and of wisdom" (Acts 6:3). Steady, wise servants of God who are hard to rattle. *Semnos*.

Later on in the New Testament, older men are told to be "dignified [*semnos*]" (Titus 2:2). Leaders are encouraged to "show integrity, dignity [*semnotes*], and sound speech" (Titus 2:7–8). Generally speaking, the Bible tells everyone to "lead a peaceful and quiet life, godly and dignified [*semnotes*] in every way" (1 Tim. 2:2). The word is even tied to parenting, as leaders are told to parent their children "with all dignity [*semnotes*]" (1 Tim. 3:4). The point is clear: the best people, the best leaders, the best parents, the best spouses somehow incorporate this aspect of thinking into their everyday lives.

This is a hard concept to pin down in one word. I'm not sure our English translations do it justice. There is so much more to the idea behind the word *semnos* than what "dignified" or "honorable" might connote.

When we consider the fullness of the historical and biblical data behind this word, we finally unveil a description of a steady person who is known for thoughtful reflection and well-reasoned, grace-filled responses to life's difficult situations. This person has some weight to their thinking, so much so that outward pressures do not move them easily. Not to be confused with someone who is stubborn or callous, this person is marked by solidity and steadiness in the way they mentally process the world around them.

When the writer of Philippians 4:8 challenges us to think about "whatever is honorable," he envisions the kind of thinking that is difficult to rattle. A person with this kind of thinking doesn't respond whimsically to the things around them and lash out. A person with this kind of mental processing knows how to keep the temperature down as things heat up around them. In short, they have a kind of thinking that is *nonreactionary*.

An Understandable Misunderstanding

At this point, you might be thinking, "Okay. I like this trait. I'm attracted to people who have it. I might even like it for myself someday. But it seems to describe a truly boring person— steady, solid, nonreactionary, staid. Where's the fun in that? I'm picturing my grandpa and Mister Rogers with a little Mother Teresa thrown in!"

Good point. And I can see how you might think this. *Semnos* is a tough concept to get our heads and hearts around. This might help: nonreactionary people still act; they just don't react in knee-jerk ways. Far from being apathetic, distant, and disengaged, nonreactionary thinkers are people with a lot of vision, tons of drive, and a core of conviction that goes right to the center of their being. It's just that they apply thoughtfulness, wisdom, and discernment *before* they act—and doing so tempers their response and sets them apart from all the craziness of popular culture.

To be sure, some of the greatest visionaries and most colorful personalities in history were nonreactionary in their thinking. Thomas Jefferson, the third president of the United States and the author of the Declaration of Independence, was extremely thoughtful in the responses he gave in regard to both internal and external issues facing his young nation. Hardly anyone ever accused him of being whimsical or reactionary—revolutionary maybe, but not reactionary. He was also an engaging conversationalist and a lover of everything outdoors. His favorite place to be was his cherished farm called Monticello, sitting high on a hill overlooking the Virginia countryside. Jefferson loved spending time at his farm, where he would shoot guns, hike, plant things, prune things, and even invent things. He would probably drive a Subaru today. Far from being a boring personality or a lifeless administrator, Jefferson was a stalwart, nonreactionary thinker who patiently faced the toughest issues of his day with life-giving wisdom, and he was the life of any party—steadiness and charisma hand in hand. Not a bad combination to have.

Likewise, Winston Churchill, the famous prime minister of Britain, shows us that one can be wise and nonreactionary without giving up drive and personality. Churchill almost single-handedly guided Britain through the ravages of World War II with incredible wisdom and thoughtfulness. His courage and timely decisiveness gave Britain (and much of Europe) the confidence and resolve to stand strong against the Nazi onslaught. His famous words "We shall never surrender" resounded for an entire generation gripped by fear and uncertainty. Steadiness and surety would clearly define much of Churchill's leadership. But Churchill was also known for his wonderful wit and sense of humor. He was a colorful personality. One-liners constantly flowed from him. And he loved cigars. He was a far cry from Mister Rogers.

History is replete with solid, visionary men and women who changed the world around them while also exhibiting an unflinching, nonreactionary way of thinking: Martin Luther King Jr., Abraham Lincoln, Joan of Arc, Sojourner Truth, William Wilberforce, just to name a few. And they were anything but boring. They had vision, conviction, and passion while simultaneously being thoughtful, steady, and nonreactionary in their thinking. A truly great combination.

Coronary Christians versus Adrenal Christians

Author and theologian John Piper wrote about the difference between what he called "coronary Christians" and "adrenal Christians," stating, "Coronary Christians are like the heart in the causes they serve. Adrenal Christians are like adrenaline—a spurt of energy and then fatigue."[2] He continued to explain that the heart is a consistent, steady muscle that keeps beating, many times without the awareness of the conscious mind, "during good days and bad days, happy and sad, high and low, appreciated and unappreciated. It never lets me down."[3] The adrenal gland, on the other hand, provides a reactionary infusion of energy—fight or flight—and then it's done. For our purposes, the heart is nonreactionary, and the adrenal gland is all about reaction. Piper concluded that we need "marathoners, not just sprinters. . . . O, for coronary Christians! Christians committed to great Causes, not great comforts. I pleaded with you to dream a dream bigger than you and your families and your churches."[4]

I must confess that one reason I am so captivated by this way of thinking is that it doesn't come naturally for me. We all have different temperaments. My temperament is feisty, energetic, extroverted, given to passion, and prone to being defensive. I tend to react to the things around me—even overreact. Ask anybody who knows me. Ask my wife. A few years ago she placed a plaque in the entryway of our house that reads, "Be nice or leave." She put it there for me. Every visitor to our house gets a kick out of it. It's a reminder for me not to get snippy and biting in my knee-jerk reactions to all that is going on around me. It's my default mode. I'm not proud of this, but it's what my fallen nature prefers.

My challenge on a daily basis is to work toward being more "coronary" in my thinking. I don't lack energy, vision, or colorfulness in my personality. I am fully capable of giving a quick and thoughtless response to just about anything thrown my way. My challenge is *not* to react so quickly and to learn to allow God's Spirit to breathe reason and truth into my soul. My challenge is to follow Jesus's path of love and others-centeredness in my responses to the things around me. "Whatever is honorable."

Progressing toward Honorable Thinking

So how do we do this? What things can you and I do to foster the kind of nonreactionary thinking that God wants for us? What steps can we take to begin to think in such a way that others might desire to be around us and even listen to us?

The Bible gives us a time-tested progression that is helpful in cultivating nonreactionary thinking. It involves three steps that build one upon another. It looks like this:

Self-Control   ⟶   Wisdom   ⟶   Steadfastness

Self-Control

As a young man, I needed a lot of self-control. I still do as a middle-aged man, but when I was younger, I really needed it. As I have already admitted, I am naturally prone to being energetic, visionary, and reactionary. As a result, one of my Achilles' heels is too quickly responding when I feel pressure. One day years ago my wife said to me, "Why don't you count to five before you respond? Give yourself a little margin before you say what you initially think." This was good advice. It's a common trick suggested by counselors and commonsense people. As I tried it, however, I found that five seconds was not nearly long enough. My mind was still swimming with some not-so-godly responses even after five seconds.

So I learned over the years to *increase* the length of time before I respond. Five seconds extended to one minute. But that wasn't enough. So one minute extended to five. Still not enough. Sometimes I need hours, even days, before I am safe to respond. My wife now calls it a "pout period." This intentional, deliberate time simply allows me to go off on my own in order to regain my composure and slow down my reactions. The Bible calls it self-control.

Today it would not be out of the norm for me to be in a meeting at work, or in a discussion with one of my adult children, or even watching the evening news and not respond right away to what is put before me. I intentionally choose to put time and space between what is coming into my head and any response I am tempted to give. Try it sometime. Carve out some time and space to process your thinking in a more rational and God-honoring way. You might feel stupid as you sit there quietly, but you actually look wise. The Bible nailed it years ago when it stated, "Everyone should be quick to listen, slow to speak and slow to become angry" (James 1:19 NIV). This is self-control in action. And it works.

The keys to experiencing self-control are twofold: time and space. In order to think in an honorable and nonreactionary way, we must intentionally create both time and space in our lives *before* we respond. This is what self-control is all about. I know this idea doesn't sound very spiritual, so let me restate it in spiritual terms: to experience self-control, we must willfully create time and space so that God's Holy

Spirit can slow us down and give us margin that allows us to think and pray about how we want to respond.

When circumstances tempt us to respond either too quickly or irrationally, self-control is our first line of defense. By definition, it keeps us under control—it keeps us from lashing out and reacting before we can give the needed thought to what we want to do or say. In this sense, self-control is not actually a thought as much as it is an action of our will. But self-control helps us create the necessary margin so we can *think* before we say or do something we might regret. Self-control is the first step—a necessary precursor—to thinking without overreacting.

Self-control is listed in the Bible as a "fruit of the Spirit" (Gal. 5:22–23). It is one of the nine primary traits of a follower of Jesus. The Bible also tells us that self-control is a "gift of God" that he gives to all who believe in him (2 Tim. 1:6–7). It's part of our spiritual DNA. The capacity for self-control is in us as people who believe in and trust the Lord. In short, there is no reason a follower of Jesus should ever lack self-control. There are no excuses. God has seen fit to give us all we need to develop and implement this trait of controlling our words and actions before we respond. Once we apply self-control, we are primed for the second step in our progression toward nonreactionary thinking: the harnessing of wisdom.

Wisdom

Now that we have used self-control to create some time and space to think, we have a perfect environment for wisdom to percolate. Wisdom is defined as applied knowledge.

Wisdom provides understanding of what to do. It is insight put into action. It is thinking that responds to a situation with the right choice.

A few years ago a friend of mine had to have a delicate surgical procedure performed on his brain. It didn't go well. During the surgery, he had a stroke that cut off oxygen to a part of his brain. As a result, he suffered permanent paralysis on the right side of his body. He has significant trouble walking and much of the time has to use a wheelchair. His speech is slurred, and he labors at times to get words out. He is in a constant state of dizziness. Most sadly, this man who loves to read and loves activities that engage the mind has trouble seeing.

Though physical therapy offered some relief at first, eventually it plateaued in what it could offer, and for the past few years, my friend has struggled with quality of life in the aftermath of his stroke. He is confined to his home most days, struggling to read, striving to carry on an extended conversation, and dealing with internal frustration much of the time. And there is only so much TV one can watch.

After a few years of this, he was beginning to give up on life. One day his wife called me and shared that he had recently gone on a hunger strike. He didn't want to live anymore and felt that the best way to go was to deprive his body of food and water. Obviously, his family was deeply concerned. So I went over for a visit. When I got there, he was not eating but was consuming some liquids. He was clearly on his way toward depriving himself of the nourishment his body needed to survive. This was indeed serious.

Over the next few weeks, I spent hours with him. We processed all that was happening to him, and I tried my pastoral best to convince him that he had a lot to live for. I mentioned his wife, his children, his grandchildren, and his friends. I called upon his faith and relationship with the Lord as reasons for him to stay until God called him home in a more natural way. I told him stories of great saints who suffered much in their later years but learned to lean on Christ for purpose and peace. I even got desperate enough to compare his life to the lives of those in more challenging situations, like Stephen Hawking, and pointed out that he still had a lot to live for and to offer the world. But none of this worked. He still wanted to die and was persistent in his determination to go without food and consume only limited liquids.

I learned years ago that my human attempts to change a person's mind and heart are limited. Since that time I have also learned that prayer is a more powerful change producer than persuasion. So I upped the ante on praying for my friend. I prayed that God would change his mind. I prayed that somehow God would give him a reason to live. I prayed that my friend would have self-control not to do anything rash. I prayed that God would give him wisdom to choose the right course of action. I prayed that God would cause him to want to live. I didn't tell my friend I was praying for him. I just prayed.

I will never forget the day, a few weeks later, when I went to visit him and could tell there had been a breakthrough. Countenance is many times a great revealer of the heart, and my friend's countenance was different. I asked him what was going on. He told me he had figured some things out. He shared that he had realized that much of his desire to die had been a combination of feeling sorry for himself mixed with a quiet anger at his wife. He told me he hadn't felt loved by her anymore and that, through a rough interchange with her, they had gotten it all out on the table. She had affirmed her love for him (sometimes masked by her own frustration with their circumstances), and they had agreed to talk things through more regularly and to affirm their love for each other. He had also agreed to be more aware of his self-pity and not allow the nagging discouragement of his disability to take him to dark places in his thinking. My friend was back in play and ready to face his future head-on.

What happened to my friend? He found life-saving wisdom. He experienced significant insight concerning both his own mental machinations (i.e., his self-pity) and the dynamic between him and his wife (i.e., his perception of being unloved and the anger that came with this). He found personal knowledge that was extremely practical to his situation. Wisdom clearly gave him the light to see his way out of a dark place, wisdom that all my persuasion was not able to give, wisdom that was aided by prayer in the shadows.

The Bible says, "If any of you lacks wisdom, let him ask God, who gives generously to all without reproach, and it will be given him" (James 1:5). It was this wisdom that allowed my friend to begin to think in a nonreactionary, honorable way. His self-control of not following through with his desire to end his life bought him time for God to give him wisdom. And wisdom delivered his soul from hasty, reactive thinking that could have resulted in a destructive, tragic outcome.

It is said that George Washington possessed a fearsome combination of reactionary passion and rare wisdom. Thomas Jefferson wrote of Washington, "His temper was naturally irritable and high toned; . . . he was most tremendous in his wrath. . . . But reflection and resolution had obtained a firm and habitual ascendency over it."[5]

Washington had learned to allow wisdom to temper his naturally reactionary response to things. This is what made him such a great leader and one of the most admired presidents in the history of America. Jefferson went on to confirm, "Perhaps the strongest feature in his character was prudence, never acting until every circumstance, every consideration was maturely weighed; refraining if he saw doubt, but, when once decided, going through with his purpose, whatever obstacles opposed."[6]

Wisdom acts this way. It's the great leveler. It takes our reactive thoughts and feelings and puts them through the filter of God's truth and grace. It causes us to make the right choices, choices that can guide a young nation to become great and choices that can bring one back from a desire not to live any longer. Wisdom is the key to learning to think in a nonreactionary way.

But one additional thing is needed to cement nonreactionary thinking: steadfastness.

Steadfastness

Steadfastness (sometimes called "perseverance") is the ability to stay sturdy. It's the ability to remain consistent. It allows a person to keep running in the race for the long haul. If steadfastness is not applied to our lives, self-control and wisdom risk being one-offs. They will be once-in-a-while activities, not mainstays. They will be adrenal, not coronary. Steadfastness is crucial to capping off the trifecta that creates nonreactionary thinking.

A great little story is tucked away in the book of Acts. It concerns a burgeoning church leader named Barnabas. In Acts 11, we find him living in Jerusalem with other church leaders. Persecution was rampant, and they were getting word daily of new start-up churches being formed by Jerusalem believers who had been scattered all over Asia Minor. They heard about one particular church in the town of Antioch that was doing well despite the persecution. They sent Barnabas to check it out. When he reached this beat-up-but-flourishing church, the first thing he noticed was that the church leaders were experiencing some phenomenal results in helping people understand Jesus. Life tends to work this way. In the midst of hardship, we also find fruit and joy. The church in Antioch was experiencing this. Then the story reveals, "When he came and saw the grace of God, he was glad, and he exhorted them all to remain faithful to the Lord *with steadfast purpose*" (Acts 11:23, emphasis added).

Sometimes little phrases that initially seem like add-ons can be significant. I believe this capstone phrase, "with steadfast purpose," is significant. Barnabas could have said to this church, "Remain faithful to the Lord," and left it at that. But he felt compelled to include the call to steadfastness. Why? I believe it's because he knew that steadfastness allows us to truly become nonreactionary in our thinking. He knew it would be easy for this persecuted church to get feisty and defensive with the surrounding culture. No one likes to be persecuted for an honestly held belief. Barnabas knew the Antioch believers had worked hard not to respond in this way but to respond with self-control and wisdom. And it was working. They were experiencing great results, as they were winning people over to a personal faith in Jesus. Being nonreactionary is a winsome trait.

But this entire scene was marked by fragility. An inherent vulnerability was rife in this volatile culture. It's why Barnabas had been sent. As Paul the apostle would find out years later, beat-up Christians are still human. They can shrink back very quickly. They can become reactionary. Their self-control and wisdom can quickly wane.

This is where steadfastness comes in on the coattails of self-control and wisdom. Steadfastness hardens the cement of what came before it with resolve and determination. Through perseverance and personal fortitude, people continue on strong and unhindered. This is why Barnabas made sure to add the call to "steadfast purpose."

When we, like the church in Antioch, hear the call to "remain faithful to the Lord *with steadfast purpose*," those added three words mean something. They remind us to stay strong. They remind us not to give up. They remind us to stay on the narrow road we have been on and to keep going no matter what. Without this call, we might be tempted to pull over to a rest stop, evaluate our journey, and maybe even turn back. Many people do this. But not those who have steadfastness. They are committed to navigating the road with self-control and wisdom.

Whatever . . .

Once again, let's dream of all the potential whatevers. What would our lives look like if we consistently responded to all the things around us with a nonreactionary kind of thinking? What would our relationships look like? What would

69

the problems at work look like? What would our runaway culture look like? What would our parenting look like? What if you and I were truly calm, cool, and collected in the midst of life's raging storms?

Maybe instead of simply admiring those rare individuals with whom we feel intimately safe (the counselor, the pastor or priest, the close friend), we would actually become such a person. Now that would be a game changer.

4

THOUGHTS THAT HEAL

Standing for True Justice

"Whatever is just . . ."

There is your brother, naked and crying! And you stand confused over the choice of an attractive floor covering.

St. Ambrose, fourth-century theologian
and church leader

I grew up in a small town about a half hour east of Cleveland, Ohio, called Chagrin Falls. It was an amazing town to live in as a kid, with its tree-lined streets, quaint shops, a town triangle complete with an old-fashioned gazebo, and a picturesque waterfall flowing right along Main Street. On the weekends, crowds of regional tourists would flock to Chagrin Falls for a stroll along the river and an ice-cream cone from the popular Popcorn Shop.

One of the things kids loved to do back then was to jump off the top of the waterfall into the deep pool below. The waterfall was about fifteen to twenty feet high, and the pool provided much-needed relief from the Ohio summer heat. The only problem was that jumping from the waterfall was illegal. For safety reasons, a local ordinance forbade "falls jumping." It wasn't a felony crime. Not even a misdemeanor. But it was a local ordinance, and the Chagrin Falls police monitored the falls fairly closely and chased away transgressing kids.

Once in a while, though, a local stuntman would light himself on fire, using a special flame-retardant suit, and jump off the falls. This was quite a show for a small town, and the spectacle attracted a sizable crowd and even local Cleveland media with plenty of cameras. As you can imagine, the police were always on hand to meet the man when he got out of the water to faithfully take him to the local station for processing. They had to be consistent with the ordinance, especially given the public nature of the stunt.

I will never forget one particular year when I was in high school. We were all standing around waiting for the stunt to begin when one of the cameramen mentioned that he would love to get a shot of someone other than the stuntman jumping off the falls. He was concerned about lighting, focus, camera angles, and all the other things professional cameramen concern themselves with. In unison, my friends all said, "Jamie will do it!" Not being shy of the spotlight, I said, "I'm in." So in front of hundreds of people, and the watching police, I climbed to the top of the falls and jumped. For the cameraman, I was a much-appreciated warm-up to the main event. It was my first experience of a crowd cheering for me. It was also my first experience with angry law enforcement.

I swam to the shore, and a Chagrin Falls policeman was there waiting for me. He looked sternly at me and said, "I have to stay on hand for the stuntman, but you're in big trouble." He then pointed to a large rock along the shore and said, "You sit right there. Don't go anywhere, and when this is all over, I'm coming back for you." He then walked away. I did as I was told, took my seat, and like a disciplined puppy, stayed put. At this point, my friends came over and to a person said, "Just go. The cop is gone. He probably won't remember you with all the excitement. Now is your chance to leave." But I had an innate respect for justice. I felt bad shunning authority (even though I have done it occasionally over the years). Something inside me said it wouldn't be a good idea to run. So I stayed put.

A few minutes later the stuntman, lit up like a human torch, jumped off the falls. The crowd went crazy. The media filmed the stunt and took pictures like they were at an inaugural parade. As anticipated, the police waited at the shore and escorted the stuntman out of the water and to the police station. And there I sat on the rock. I assumed they would eventually come back for me. The policeman had told me to stay put. He had told me not to go anywhere. So I sat there for what seemed like an eternity. Eventually, my friends left (a testament to friendship). Then it started getting dark. Most of the people were gone. And there I sat on the rock. I sat there for at least an hour.

I didn't know what to do. I thought about heading to the police station and turning myself in. I didn't want to be on Chagrin Falls's Top Ten Most Wanted list. But turning myself in felt like overkill. Falls jumping was akin to a parking ticket in my hometown. Few people ever turned themselves in for parking in front of an expired meter. But justice is justice. Right is right and wrong is wrong. So there I sat.

Eventually, everyone was gone. The shops closed up. The nighttime stars began singing their nightly song. And the policeman did not return. Like Bill Murray slinking away from the golf course he blew up at the end of the movie *Caddyshack*, I looked around and apprehensively began walking home. The police never put out a warrant for my arrest. To this day, I guess I am a fugitive on the run.

Our Innate Sense for Justice

Unless you are what psychologists call a "sociopath," you almost surely have something inside you that at least *agrees* with justice. You might not always abide by this innate sense, but you mostly *agree* with it. The Bible calls this sense a "conscience" (see Rom. 2:15). Murderers deserve punishment. Cheaters should be held accountable. Liars should be found out and exposed. Speeders should get a ticket. The human soul is hardwired for justice. It's what allows us to get along in a civilized society. It's what causes you and me to think in categories of right and wrong, good and bad—and to cheer for what is right and good. It's why action movies always have a hero (someone who fights for the good) and why great fiction consistently has a protagonist and an antagonist. We inwardly long for the good to win the day and feel offended and scandalized when injustice wins the day. It's also what keeps a teenage boy sitting on a rock waiting for a policeman to return.

The mindset of justice is included in God's top eight list of how to think. It's at the core of a right perspective in life.

Like many things in life, however, justice is easily agreed with but not always understood. We have an innate sense for it, but we don't always know what it entails. For instance, how do we know what is actually right and wrong? What should our standard be? And once we discern these things, what should we do to right the wrongs of this world? Where do forgiveness and mercy come into play? And who decides? There is a lot more to justice than initially meets the eye.

"Whatever Is Just"

Unlike the rare word we looked at in the previous chapter, the Greek word for justice is a very common one. It's the word *dikaios* (pronounced *dih-KAI-ahs*), and it was used literally thousands of times by the Greco-Roman writers of Jesus's day. The Greeks were on the cutting edge of social engineering. They had sophisticated cities, elaborate marketplace centers, and state-of-the-art educational academies. They excelled in commerce and military power. And though not always just in their decisions and actions, they at least prized justice as fundamental to societal and individual morality.

The word *dikaios* refers to what is morally right, correct, and good. It can even be used to describe a person as morally "innocent"[1]—on the right side of justice. Plato used this word to refer to "inner order"[2]—the order of the mind as it discerns what is right and good. This concept of justice was central for the Greeks in developing a disciplined and proper way of thinking. The idea was that a right and just way of thinking would lead to a right and proper way of behaving. Mind over body.

Rationality and philosophical reasoning were crucial for the Greeks in developing *dikaios*. In short, they believed in thinking their way through to a workable standard for justice. Aristotle wrote an entire book on ethics that was based on philosophical and rational foundations.[3] It was used for centuries during the Middle Ages (even by some Christian theologians) as a textbook for what was right and just. Many people in our highly developed, post-Christian, Enlightenment-based society here in the West have adopted a similar way of functioning. They utilize rationality and pragmatism (i.e., what works) as the basis for justice. If something seems right to an inquiring mind, then it must be right.

As good and fine as this approach might be, it contains an inherent weakness. Ethics and justice based solely on rationality and philosophical inquiry, void of any other basis, can easily become relative. Justice becomes only as good as one's particular reasoning and certainly not universally applicable to all. Ethics become entrenched in a culture, as that culture tends to agree on a particular approach and basis for justice, but not transferable to others. In other words, what might seem rational to one group of people in a particular time and place might not be rational to another group living in a different time or place.

The mere fact that the Greek version of justice is not utilized by most major people groups today is evidence of this. It worked well for the Greeks, but then other cultures developed their own basis for justice and what is right. Even closer to home, much of the world has a different form of justice than the United States. Many cultures in the West utilize an Enlightenment-based standard for justice, while some Middle Eastern cultures opt for Sharia law. It's hard to arrive at a universally agreed-upon standard for what is right. And this makes justice a hard thing to measure and apply.

As was noted earlier, we each have an innate sense of justice, but what the basis and foundation for this should be is not clear. This is not to suggest that philosophical reasoning is a completely faulty approach. The Greeks found it helpful, and their culture existed for centuries as a result. Their approach just doesn't go far enough. There has to be more to this idea of *dikaios* if it is to have broad and universal appeal. Thankfully, there is more.

By This Standard

When the biblical writers wrote about justice, they used this common Greek word *dikaios*. They didn't change the definition. They didn't mess with its meaning. And they certainly didn't shy away from this word. The Greek version of the Old Testament, called the Septuagint, contains more than four hundred occurrences of this word. The New Testament writers used it more than eighty times. We shouldn't be surprised that the Bible talks about justice and what is morally right. What the biblical writers did with this word, however, was revolutionary. They added a key ingredient to the secular foundation that acted as a hardening agent to the biblical understanding. This ingredient made the foundation sure and solid in its timelessness and not subject to the shifting values of changing times and cultures. That key ingredient was God.

When we look closely at all the uses of *dikaios* in the Bible, it becomes clear that God's revelation, his character, and his law are the solid foundation for what is just and right, not merely the prevailing thoughts and values of a given people at a given time. The Bible cements justice in the eternal person of God himself. The standard is God. This standard should be the basis of our thinking concerning justice. Philosophical reasoning is still in play, for we have to use our rational minds to understand God's revelation, character, and law. We also have to wrestle mentally with how God's call to justice should play out in our daily pursuit of justice. But we are no longer relying on rationality alone as the basis for our understanding of justice. A theistic foundation changes everything.

Consider God's character—who he is as a person. Psalm 116:5 declares, "Gracious is the LORD, and righteous [*dikaios*]." In Revelation 16:5 an angel says of God, "Just [*dikaios*] are you, O Holy One, who is and who was, for you brought these judgments." Justice is rooted in God's character and being, his eternal, unchanging, trinitarian character. Because God is just and good, he is the foundation of our justice and goodness. We are to be good because God is good. We are to understand justice in light of the character of God, who himself is just.

But our understanding of justice doesn't stop there. The Bible goes on to declare specifically what is just and right, and it flows from God's revelation and law. Romans 7:12 states, "So the law is holy, and the commandment is holy and righteous [*dikaios*] and good." Romans 2:13 echoes something similar when it reports, "For it is not the hearers of the law who are righteous before God, but the doers of the law who will be justified." Jesus affirmed this too when he said, "If you love me, you will keep my commandments. . . . Whoever has my commandments and keeps them, he it is who loves me" (John 14:15, 21). God loves us enough to let us know what he thinks about us and this world. This is why he gave us his law and commands. His revelation, contained in the Bible, is the very foundation of how we are to think about justice. Everything from the Ten Commandments to the socially reforming words of the prophets to the society-shaping implications of the Beatitudes of Jesus to the moral imperatives of the New Testament Epistles now informs and guides what true justice and righteousness should look like.

So how do we know what is right and just? What is the standard of justice? It is found in the character and the revelation of God. It is found in everything the Bible says about him and what he has said to us in the Bible. Grounding justice in far more than what our rational minds might consider, God declares himself and his Word to be the foundation. Accordingly, fixing focus on the possibilities of God's justice has brought healing and hope to countless people who had suffered under the injustices of what was otherwise acceptable and permissible. For centuries, this foundation has guided God's people—through all kinds of settings and cultures—and given us a universal and absolute standard of justice. The famous Nobel Peace Prize winner Archbishop Desmond Tutu put it this way: "There's nothing more radical, nothing more revolutionary, nothing more subversive against injustice and oppression than the Bible. If you want to keep people subjugated, the last thing you place in their hands is a Bible."[4]

Let's Get Radical

What the Bible says about how we are to use God's sense of justice in response to the injustice of this world is both challenging and life giving. At first glance, it seems oxymoronic. The two primary things the Bible tells us to do seem to go in different directions—even polar-opposite directions. But if learning to think about "whatever is just" is about developing thoughts that heal by bringing joy to ourselves and others, then these two will do the trick. Here is what the Bible says:

Think justice → Doing right through righting wrongs
Think justice → Making right through forgiving wrongs

We are to *do* right and to *make* right. One involves the pursuit of righting wrongs through our just actions. The other involves the choice to forgive injustice and thus help free people who do wrong to become right. Let's take a look at each one.

Thinking Right Leads to Doing Right

One thing I love about the Bible is how often it calls us to do right in order to right wrongs. We are to "think justice." This involves having a daily mindset that is about discerning, assessing, and responding. We are to discern what things are not just (or what should be just) according to the standard of God's Word. We are then to assess what we can and should do to bring justice to the world around us. Then we are to respond accordingly. Discern. Assess. Respond. When these three things are a part of our daily mental arsenal, we are bound to make an impact. As Mark Twain said so well, "Do the right thing. It will gratify some people and astonish the rest."[5]

Let's do the math. There are more than seven billion people in the world. Of these, almost one-third claim the label "Christian." This means there are more than two billion people in the world who would be interested in thinking about what is just according to God's character and revelation. Add to this the number of people who are generally theistic and sensitive to the things of the Bible, and the number swells. Arguably, half of the world's population might be open to God's version of justice. Now imagine if each of these individuals adopted just one area in which to do right in order to right a wrong. Just one. Obviously, we can't cure every ill, but each of us can adopt one particular area. Imagine the impact we would make. Imagine the healing that would occur. Upward of three billion people who each make it their lifelong vision to pursue just one area of doing right through righting a wrong would be a literal army of justice seekers. We would be an unstoppable force of love in a fallen world that has so many wounded. We would turn thoughts that heal into a multitude of actions that would sing a beautiful song of justice. The young people in our culture call this being "missional." Imagine if every Christian was "on mission" in one particular area in this needy world of ours.

In the over a quarter of a century that I have interacted with and observed many good-hearted justice seekers, their particular areas of focus have blown me away. Here is a sample:

poverty	immigration	literacy
hunger	sex trafficking	bullying
health care	seniors/aging	mental illness
homelessness	religious liberty	peacekeeping
orphans	racism	environmentalism
prisoner care	women's rights	civil rights

foster care/adoption	hatred	community
unwed mothers	volunteerism	development
battered women	financial generosity	urban renewal
refugees	street kids	crime
		substance abuse

This is just a sampling. There are so many areas to which we can bring justice by righting wrongs. So what is your area?

A few years ago I preached a sermon on kindness. My point was that if Christians could learn to be kind to those around them, this might make a huge difference in their love and impact. I referenced 1 Corinthians 13:4, which says, "Love is . . . kind." One imaginative woman in my church began thinking about what this could look like in her life. She was burdened by all the unkindness that goes on in our schools. She wanted to try to right this wrong by reinforcing the value of kindness to kids in schools. Taking some of the time, talents, and treasures that God had blessed her and her husband with, she started "The Be Kind People Project." Its straightforward mission is to ask young people to take "The Be Kind Pledge." By doing so, they commit to ten core values of kindness that include being encouraging, being supportive, being helpful, and being honest.

What began as a passion for justice ballooned quickly. This woman and a committed core of volunteers who agreed with her conviction to be kind developed a nonprofit organization that puts on school assemblies, hands out "Classroom Kindness Kits," sponsors youth leadership conferences, and engages in teacher appreciation sessions. It is now a nationwide movement that has produced some impressive results. Volunteers have delivered twenty-eight million classroom resources nationwide, put on over three hundred school assemblies, and influenced five million students.[6] All this from the passion of one woman who heard God's call for justice.

I wonder what God might want to do through you.

Christians have a long and storied history with this kind of justice. A few years ago the media was highlighting some of the hypocrisy that exists among vocal Christians. This kind of reporting is a regular occurrence in our culture— sometimes fair and sometimes not so fair. Nevertheless, a watching world sees and notes what we do. In this particular wave of criticism, however, Nicholas Kristof, a two-time Pulitzer Prize–winning journalist for the *New York Times*, wrote an op-ed in which he said this in defense of Christians and their work in righting wrongs:

> Evangelicals are disproportionately likely to donate 10 percent of their incomes to charities, mostly church-related. More important, go to the front lines, at home or abroad, in the battles against hunger, malaria, prison rape, obstetric fistula, human trafficking or genocide, and some of the bravest people you meet are evangelical Christians (or conservative Catholics, similar in many ways) who truly live their faith. I'm not particularly religious myself, but I stand in awe of those I've seen risking their lives in this way—and it sickens me to see that faith mocked at New York cocktail parties.[7]

We are to "think justice." We are to have thoughts that heal and bring joy. When we think in this way and act upon our thoughts, God moves in response. He does his kingdom-building work here on earth. People are touched.

The Other Side of Justice

The second way we are to "think justice" is by making right through forgiving wrongs. I call this "the other side of justice." It sure feels this way. It is the seeming opposite of how we think justice should be applied. It taps into God's grace and mercy. It recognizes that God's justice is not one-dimensional but multifaceted. When we pursue justice in this way, we choose not just the consequential side of justice but also the forgiveness side.

There is a clear and wonderful logic to this side of God's justice. When God thinks about you and me and what is just, he begins with this observation: "None is righteous; no, not one" (Rom. 3:10). In other words, we each fall short in our lives compared to what God's original design for us was. We all fall short of God's standard (what the Bible calls his "law"). Because God is just, the consequence of our sin is separation from him, now and for all eternity. God is holy. Sin is an affront to his holiness. Justice demands separation.

But justice can be meted out in various ways. In light of sin, a consequence has to ensue for there to be justice, but this consequence can take different forms. This is where Jesus comes in. Instead of giving us the consequence for our sin, God sent Jesus. The Bible says it this way: "For our sake he [God] made him [Jesus] to be sin who knew no sin, so that in him we might become the righteousness of God" (2 Cor. 5:21). Jesus gave his life through his death on a cross so that we might be forgiven. He bore our sin upon himself so that we might be cleansed of sin in God's sight. And for those who place their faith and trust in Jesus, God applies Jesus's death on their behalf and forgives them of their sin. Justice is accomplished. However, it is accomplished through forgiveness. "It was to show his righteousness at the present time, so that he might be just and the justifier of the one who has faith in Jesus" (Rom. 3:26).

Forgiveness is an unlikely path to justice but one that truly heals, especially when we are stuck in our fallen ways and need the freedom that only forgiveness can provide. Freedom to begin a new day. Freedom to let past offenses go. Freedom to stop looking in the rearview mirror at the road of our mistakes and mishaps and begin to look forward to the road ahead, a road filled with lots of whatevers. Forgiveness as justice. Who would have thought? God did.

God then turns the tables on us. In light of thinking about "whatever is just," the Bible commands, "Be kind to one another, tenderhearted, forgiving one another, as God in Christ forgave you" (Eph. 4:32). Just as God applies justice in the form of forgiveness, we are commanded to do so as well. We are told to forgive and, in this way, promote justice.

Why Not Both/And?

Have you ever noticed that most people, even most Christians, tend to be good at *either* righting wrongs *or* forgiving wrongs? I know individuals who are disciplined, fair-minded, just people; and I know individuals who are tenderhearted, loving, forgiving people. But I don't know too many who are both. I don't know many people who seek to right wrongs while simultaneously offering the olive branch of forgiveness for those same wrongs. It's true that the two actions don't seem to go together. As we have seen, however, with God, they do. And with us, they should.

Could it be that thoughts that heal dare to bring the two together? This is a bold idea. Even bolder is applying them. Both/and rather than either/or looks like this:

- a Christian who campaigns for an end to drunk driving while forgiving drunk drivers
- a Christian who fights for the rights of the unborn while forgiving those who have abortions
- a Christian who believes marriage should be between a man and a woman while befriending, accepting, and journeying with gay couples
- a Christian who works with the poor while forgiving all the materialists in our society

These are radical scenarios. Our world hardly ever sees these dual expressions of justice in the same individual. But when it does, people are blown away. Martin Luther King Jr. fought bravely for equality yet lived a life of love toward all people—even racists and bigots. Mother Teresa devoted her life to ministering to the poorest of the poor in India yet interacted gently and patiently with wealthy capitalists from the West. Some of the greatest activists in history were individuals who had the unique ability to both right wrongs and forgive wrongs.

You and I have so many opportunities in our daily lives to "think justice." Imagine if we approached each daily opportunity with the dual mindset of doing right and making right—of righting wrongs and forgiving wrongs. Our actions would change the world. At the very least, they would turn heads. And joy would be ours.

"Whatever is just . . . think about these things."

5

THE MYTH OF
INDIVIDUAL HOLINESS

A Relational Approach to Purity

"Whatever is pure . . ."

People have no idea what one saint can do: for sanctity is
stronger than the whole of hell.

Thomas Merton

I was not raised in a very religious home. We didn't go to
church often. We were what I call "CEO Christians," meaning "Christmas-Easter-Only Christians." We didn't read the
Bible as a family. I never saw my mom or dad read it. We
didn't talk about religious or spiritual things. We did say a
short blessing before dinner, but it didn't mean much to me
as a kid. Don't get me wrong, my upbringing was moral and
loving, just not overtly religious. My parents came from good

Midwestern stock. They taught me and my siblings manners and respect and instilled in us a strong work ethic. We were all college bound, because education was the key to success. It was a typical Norman Rockwell, American home.

As a young adult, I had a profound spiritual experience that led me to faith in Jesus Christ. One could say I was "born again" in the way Jesus originally used the phrase (see John 3:3–7). I understood that God existed, that sin separated me from him (I had eighteen years of empirical evidence to back that up), and that Jesus was and is the one who came to bring me to God through faith in his sacrificial death on a cross for my sins. As I have said often over the years, my spiritual life went from black-and-white to Technicolor when I understood and accepted the gospel.

I quickly immersed myself in the Christian subculture. I started going to church. I joined a couple of Bible studies. I tuned in to Christian radio teachers. I read theological books. I even listened to contemporary Christian music. As a result of all this, I started hearing an entirely new vocabulary that was foreign to my secular ears. People asked me if I was "saved." They called me "brother." We sang songs in church, but we didn't call them songs; instead, they were "hymns" and "choruses." When the pastor spoke, it was called a "sermon." The pastor talked about "the blood of the Lamb," which "atoned" for my sin. I soon realized this subculture had a language all its own, a language I would eventually learn to speak.

One of the words I was exposed to early on was the word *holy*. Christians used it to describe both God and people. It was a positive term. A complimentary one. It wasn't a word I had heard or used often in the world in which I had grown up. The only time I had ever heard that word before was as an adjective: "Holy moly" (or with a more crass noun following it). I would soon learn, however, that this word is one of the most important words in learning to think as a follower of God.

"Whatever Is Pure"

The next line of thought as we journey through Philippians 4:8 invites us to think about "whatever is pure." This fascinating word, pregnant with thought-provoking meaning, is the Greek word *hagnos* (pronounced *hawg-NAHS*), and it is translated as "pure; undefiled; innocent; holy."[1] And behind the veil of this word is both a brilliant concept and a life-changing call.

Hagnos is the cousin of the primary word for "holy" in the New Testament, *hagios* (pronounced *HA-ghee-ahs*). "Holy" means to be set apart. It means to set something or someone aside in how we see and treat them, away from all the things that might tarnish them. When we call God "holy," we are separating him in our minds from all the things that aren't God (which is everything within creation) and casting him in an entirely different light. This is the idea behind Revelation 4:8 when it says, "Holy, holy, holy, is the Lord God Almighty." God is "almighty" (mighty in a way that no one else is), so he is called "holy." We separate God in our perspective based on his unique and unequaled attributes, and we call him "holy." It should not surprise us, then, that this is a common word in the Bible. The Bible talks about God. God is set apart for so many reasons. God is holy. The Bible uses the word *holy* just shy of one thousand times!

The word *holy* is also sometimes used to describe people in the Bible. As you might imagine, this use is rare compared to when the word refers to God. And though the primary word for "holy" (*hagios*) is used of people in the Bible at times, the closely related word *hagnos* is used exclusively to describe certain people. Used eight times in the New Testament, *hagnos* carries with it the idea of wholeness and integrity. It is translated "pure" because it is used to describe people who exhibit a level of behavior and relating that is not being compromised by the world around them. Like the primary word for "holy," this word still means "set apart," but it does so in the sense that someone is relatively unstained or undiluted by all the negative influences around them. This is the conceptual idea behind the word *pure*.

Where this word gets traction, however, is in its actual uses in the New Testament. How it is used forms the life-changing call that *hagnos* gives us.

Personal and Relational

When we examine the eight uses of the word *pure* in the New Testament, we see that they fall neatly into two distinct buckets: personal and relational. In other words, *hagnos* is used to describe either personal purity or a purity that is seen only as we interact relationally with those around us. In some cases, it describes both. Let's examine each bucket.

On a personal level, followers of Jesus are called to be pure in their behavior and conduct. Paul told Timothy, "Do not be hasty in the laying on of hands, nor take part in the sins of others; keep yourself pure [*hagnos*]" (1 Tim. 5:22). This idea was affirmed by Peter when he wrote to women who were trying to be good examples to their unbelieving husbands. Peter said they would be won over "when they see your respectful and pure [*hagnos*] conduct" (1 Pet. 3:2). The Greek version of the Old Testament sums up this idea best when it says, "The way of the guilty is crooked, but the conduct of the pure [*hagnos*] is upright" (Prov. 21:8). Each of these verses uses this concept of purity on a *personal* level. They refer to a believer's conduct—the actions and behaviors they are to have. Our actions are to be unstained and "set apart" from the immoral craziness of the world around us. We show our purity in everything from our words to our sexuality to our honesty to our business ethics—anything that has to do with our personal morality. Many of us associate this concept with holiness. We are to mimic the righteousness and set-apart nature of God himself.

But this is only half the story. Another equally important aspect of this call involves how we interact with those around us, how we *relate*. James 3:17 lists relational traits that define what true wisdom looks like. It says, "But the wisdom from above is first pure [*hagnos*], then peaceable, gentle, open to reason, full of mercy and good fruits, impartial and sincere." These are all relational traits. They are interactional in nature. You can't demonstrate these traits without other people. Being peaceable, gentle, open to reason, merciful, impartial, and sincere all involve interacting with others. They are never found in isolation from others. And "pure" (*hagnos*) is listed as "first."

Paul the apostle used this word in a similar way. When he was writing to the church in Corinth, at one point he spoke intimately with them. He wrote about his own hardships and difficulties as a follower of Jesus. He pointed out that the "coming of Titus" provided great comfort to him (2 Cor. 7:6). Relationships can do this. They can provide comfort and assurance when we need them most. God designed them to be this way. Paul then went on to let the Corinthians know that their presence in his life was a great source of comfort to him as well. In light of others who had hurt him, Paul added, "At every point you have proved yourselves innocent [*hagnos*] in the matter" (2 Cor. 7:11). Paul was thankful for the purity (innocence) of the Corinthians. It was a purity displayed in their *relationship* with him. It was seen in how they treated him.

Two buckets. One to contain the call to be pure in our conduct on a personal level; the other to contain the call to be pure in our relational interactions with others. The word before us is used as a call to both. The above instances clearly show this. Holiness is just as much a relational characteristic as it is a personal one. Most people tend to view holiness and purity as individual projects. They are seen as something you achieve and display between you and God—and only between you and God. This is a myth. Holiness and purity were always designed to include a strong relational component.

So which call is given in Philippians 4:8? What does *hagnos* mean when we are told to think about "whatever is pure"? The context doesn't tell us. The verse tells us to think this way, but it's one of those rare verses that doesn't say whether this purity is personal or relational. In the absence of any contextual clues, combined with the fact that the concept appears in a generic list, we can only assume that the fullness of *hagnos*, in both its personal and its relational setting, must be in play. Bottom line: the call to think about "whatever is pure" means that we are to be good and relate well. These form the defining characteristics of our holiness.

Becoming "Little Christs"

C. S. Lewis once gave an immense challenge to Christians to become what he called "little Christs." He said:

> Now the whole offer which Christianity makes is this: that we can, if we let God have his way, come to share in the life of Christ. If we do, we shall then be sharing a life which was begotten, not made, which always has existed and always will exist. Christ is the Son of God. If we share in this kind of life we also shall be sons of God. We shall love the Father as he does and the Holy Ghost will arise in us. He came to this world and became a man in order to spread to other men the kind of life he has—by what I call "good infection." Every Christian is to become a little Christ. The whole purpose of becoming a Christian is simply nothing else.[2]

I like this challenge: becoming a "little Christ." Obviously, Lewis didn't mean that we become little Messiahs or little perfect incarnate sons of God. That would be taking this idea too far. What he meant is that we need to grow more and more like Jesus in our daily walk with him. We need to emulate the way Jesus trusted in God the Father and the way Jesus interacted with those around him, the way he loved them. Becoming a "little Christ" means living and loving the way Jesus did. It means patterning our lives after the relational interactions of Jesus presented in the Gospels.

This is the same idea author Larry Crabb was after when he wrote that the goal of our purity is attained by "bringing God's relational Kingdom to earth by becoming increasingly relationally holy—by Christians learning to put Christ's way of relating on display first to each other and then overflowing with Jesus-like love to the world."[3] Imagine if every Christian "put Christ's way of relating on display" in their everyday lives. What would happen if Christians dared to see their holiness as measured not solely by their personal, moral choices but by each and every relational interaction they had? This would take our sanctification to an entirely new level. Each and every day would be a journey of victories and defeats measured not by our personal holiness alone but by our relational holiness as well. Every relational interaction we had, small or big, would count in the sight of God. All day long, each would either contribute to or detract from our holiness and purity.

Think about all the interactions we have in our everyday lives that would contribute to or detract from our holiness:

- how we respond to our spouse at the end of a long day
- how we relate to our kids when they are acting out
- how we handle the service provider who frustrates us with their subpar performance
- how we deal with conflict with a boss or a teacher who is being unreasonable and unfair
- how we treat the person in our small group who is clearly an EGRP (Extra-Grace-Required Person)
- how we view the rude driver on the freeway

When we consider how Jesus might have responded in each of these scenarios, the challenge becomes clear. The possibilities of "whatever is pure" become apparent.

A few years ago it was popular to wear a WWJD (What Would Jesus Do?) bracelet. These bracelets were all the rage.

They reminded us to live our lives with a personal morality that mimicked that of the Savior. A focus on *relational holiness*, however, is an entirely different level. We would need an HWJR bracelet: How Would Jesus Relate? It might not have the same ring to it, but it gets the point across. Purity in action. Purity in *interaction*.

"Love Is . . ."

I have a friend who has been wildly successful in business. Early in his career, he got involved in the engineering of plastics. Though some might not find this kind of endeavor very interesting, my friend did extremely well. He eventually sold his business for a lot of money. With a stable income for the rest of his life, he retired early and set out to find what God had next for him.

Amid his search to identify what God intended next for him, some thoughts became clear. He didn't want to spend his remaining days doing only philanthropy. Though he and his wife gave generously to numerous nonprofit organizations, he wanted to have a personal imprint on the fabric of family and relationships. Because he had spent much of his adult years overly focused on his business, the quality of his most important relationships had suffered. He wanted to reverse this trend and devote the rest of his life to building strong and healthy family relationships and other close relationships.

His journey to discover what God wanted most for him gave him the desire to know what really matters. As he read the Bible with a more open mind and a desire to hone in on what is most important, he realized that relational love is the obvious goal. He realized that once a person has come to faith in Christ, relational love becomes the barometer of their sanctification (see Matt. 22:36–39; John 13:34; 1 Cor. 13:13; 1 Tim. 1:5).

First Corinthians 13 is commonly known as the "Love Chapter." It extols both the virtues and the centrality of what it means to love God and others. At one point, it says this:

> Love is patient and kind; love does not envy or boast; it is not arrogant or rude. It does not insist on its own way; it is not irritable or resentful; it does not rejoice at wrongdoing, but rejoices with the truth. Love bears all things, believes all things, hopes all things, endures all things. Love never ends. (vv. 4–8)

My friend decided to rewrite this verse by taking out the word *love* and inserting his own name. His logic was that if God calls us to a life of relational love as a way of showing that we are followers of Jesus, then we can put our own name in place of the word *love* as a way to gauge whether we are truly being loving. Using my name, it reads like this:

- Jamie is patient and kind.
- Jamie does not envy or boast.
- Jamie is not arrogant or rude.
- Jamie does not insist on his own way.
- Jamie is not irritable or resentful.
- Jamie does not rejoice at wrongdoing but rejoices with the truth.
- Jamie bears all things, believes all things, hopes all things, endures all things.
- Jamie never ends (in his quest for relational love).

As my friend went through his day, he would periodically take out this rewritten verse to see how it compared to his relational responses to all that was going on around him. He applied it to how he treated his wife, his children, his grandchildren, his friends, the person working in his yard, the kid at McDonald's taking his order, the people in his small group at church—anyone he interacted with. He even went so far as to develop a personal app for his phone that allowed him to rate himself on a scale of 1 to 10 at the end of each day for each of his relational responses. Most gutsy, he would ask his wife to help him with this.

After a few months of doing this daily, he shared with me that this task was both exciting and daunting. There were times he would give himself a solid eight or nine for a particular relational interaction, and then there were times he would have to give himself a three or four. He regularly lifted his sights upward and asked God for help. He called him "Coach." He would say, "Coach, I need some help here. I want to relate like Jesus, but it's beyond my reach. I need you to love this person through me" (see Gal. 2:20). Each day became an exciting adventure in learning to put Christ on display in the way he related.

My friend's newfound pursuit of relational love is something I wish every Christ follower had. I'm not suggesting we all need to utilize a homemade app to track our relational holiness. My friend is an engineer by trade and has a dramatic flair for precision and analytics. But if every follower of Jesus had a similar passion and a similar daily commitment, there would be no stopping us. Every day would be an endless stream of whatevers in regard to relational holiness expressed in Jesus-like love.

Trendy Evangelicals

Evangelical Christians tend to be a trendy group of people. Grounded in a belief in personal salvation through faith in Jesus, which is built upon an uncompromising commitment to the Bible, they are good at responding to the culture around them. These responses quickly become trends. And trends are both good and bad. They are helpful and hurtful. Each decade for the past fifty years has seen a different trend for Christians in America.

Back in the 1970s, the trend was eschatology. It was sparked by Hal Lindsey's bestselling book, *The Late Great Planet Earth*. Chronicling the Bible's numerous prophetic predictions, this book outlined what could happen as the end of time approaches, complete with the second coming of Jesus Christ preceded by a great tribulation and a rapture of all believers. With two devastating world wars recently behind us, the continual Cold War with Russia, the worldwide oil crisis, and the turmoil in the Middle East, our nation was ripe for a focus on God's ultimate eschatological plan for this world. Lindsey's book eventually sold over thirty-five million copies and was made into a full-length motion picture narrated by Orson Welles.[4] Many Americans remember this trend. In great part it's what evangelicals were known for in the decade of the seventies.

In the 1980s, the culture wars began, and the trend switched to politics. The Moral Majority was formed. Its goal was to speak conservative, Christian values loudly and clearly into the political realm. Ronald Reagan was elected president and wrote a book opposing abortion. Following Jimmy Carter, a self-described "born-again Christian," Reagan likewise was sympathetic to evangelicals' values. This decade saw the rise of powerful organizations such as Focus on the Family, the American Family Association, and the Christian Coalition. These groups and many more were designed to combat increasing secularism in the public arena. And politics was the primary arena. Liberty University became fully established by 1984, and its founder, Jerry Falwell, became a strong voice for Christian values. Regardless of what you might think of all this, evangelicals penetrated partisan politics in a way that had not been seen in the history of our nation. Much of the eighties was consumed with the rise of evangelical politics. As two respected researchers summarize, "Beginning in the 1980s and continuing into the first decade of the new century, conservative politics became the most visible aspect of religion in America."[5]

In keeping with the trendy nature of our modern world, a new trend for evangelicals arose in the 1990s. It was the rise of the seeker-sensitive megachurch movement. A megachurch is defined as a church with two thousand or more attendees. Before 1970, only a handful of megachurches existed in the United States. The latest count is 1,667 megachurches,[6] and many of these arose in the 1990s. Even more dramatic is a 2012 study that revealed that one in ten churchgoers in America attend a megachurch.[7] There are almost 314,000 Protestant churches in America,[8] and yet 10 percent of churchgoers attend one-half of 1 percent of those churches. What draws people to a megachurch? This question has a complicated answer. Full-service programs; band-driven worship environments; well-honed, practical sermons; intimate small group offerings; and well-equipped, college-size campuses all contribute to the attraction of megachurches for millions of Americans. In addition, cultural changes contributed to this phenomenon. Walmart, Home Depot, Lowes, and Super Kmart—what we call the "big box" stores—attracted consumers to a one-stop shopping experience. Churches followed suit. Since the vast majority of churches in America are not "mega" in size, only time will tell what the future of these very large churches will be. One thing is for sure though: millions flocked to them in the 1990s, creating a significant trend among Christians in America.

Around the turn of the century, a new trend began. It is known as the "missional movement." In contrast to the long-standing "attractional" church, the missional church argued that we are not to wait for people to come to us; rather, as "sent ones," we are to go to them.[9] The church is to be present in culture similar to how Jesus was out and about in Palestine in the first century. Holing up in church buildings and waiting for others to darken our doors is not the Jesus way. Being on mission out in culture is. This movement has garnered much support from younger evangelicals. From setting up worship environments in coffee shops to bettering communities through social justice initiatives, the missional approach to spreading the love of Jesus has been a much-needed corrective within our church-saturated American culture. It's a trend that continues to bear much fruit.

The Love Trend

Why all this talk about trends? Why trace the things that Christians have emphasized in the past four-plus decades? Doing so goes back to something I mentioned earlier: trends are both good and bad. Trends are good, as they tend to restore balance to the things that have gotten out of whack. They garner unity and get us focused. They get a group of people going in the same direction, hopefully a good one. But because trends by their very nature are current and centered around preferences, they come and go. They last for a season, and then it's on to the next thing. And though this might be fine with certain things like clothing fashion and hairstyles, it can be counterproductive when it comes to much more significant things.

Here's my fear: there is good reason to believe that relational love is fast becoming the new trend among present-day Christians. Though I don't have solid empirical evidence for this belief, my sense is that this is the case. My current library is filled with dozens of new books—written by seasoned Christian authors—extolling the virtues of love in the form of relationality. The talk among many well-respected pastors and Christian leaders is love. Many churches are beginning to challenge their people to pursue loving relationships and loving actions. And this is good. I'm thrilled that the central focus of Jesus's call to us is now getting the due attention it deserves as this new trend picks up steam. It wouldn't surprise me if we look back on the second decade of this century and label it the decade of love.

However, should love be a trend? As we have noted, trends come and go. It's part of their nature. Should relational love follow the same trajectory of a decade of emphasis and then a loss of influence as we move on to the next latest and greatest thing? Should it follow the same pathway in our modern culture as eschatology, politics, megachurches, and being missional? I certainly hope not. It's too central to God's economy to be relegated to the level of a trend. Relational love is too much at the heart of God, and too fundamental to how we are to function as followers of Jesus, to be added to a list of twentieth- and twenty-first-century evangelical-style statements.

Thinking about "whatever is pure" is one of God's top eight ways of thinking. Living out purity in the form of relational holiness is not intended to be trendy. My hope is that as you and I cement this call to relational holiness in our minds and hearts, we will buck the trend. It is my hope that we will live the rest of our lives giving much daily thought to "whatever is pure."

6

CHRISTIAN HEDONISTS

Why You Should Pursue Pleasure

"Whatever is lovely . . ."

No one can live without delight and that is why a man deprived of spiritual joy goes over to carnal pleasures.

Thomas Aquinas

Everyone loves pleasure. There isn't one person who doesn't love some sort of pleasure. We love the pleasure of a good friend or a nice vacation. We love the pleasure of a good day at work. We love the pleasure of a good meal. We love the pleasure of our spouses and children. We love the pleasure of a beautiful piece of art or a breathtaking scene of nature. Some of us even love the pleasure of a really good sermon! We find many things in life to be great sources of pleasure. *Merriam-Webster's Collegiate Dictionary* defines pleasure as "a state of gratification; a source of delight or joy."[1] The human soul is arguably hardwired to run, in great part, on the fuel of pleasure.

The founders of our country certainly thought so. The Declaration of Independence states, "We hold these truths to be self-evident, that all men are created equal, that they are endowed by their Creator with certain unalienable Rights, that among these are Life, Liberty, and the pursuit of Happiness." That's pleasure. Even the great Westminster Confession agrees. After it asks the question "What is the chief end of man?" it answers with, "Man's chief end is to glorify God and to enjoy him forever." That's pleasure.

"Whatever Is Lovely"

We shouldn't be surprised, then, that this idea of pleasure is in God's top eight list of things that should form our daily mindset. Philippians 4:8 declares, "Whatever is lovely . . . think about these things."

At first glance, we might not see anything in this sentence that encourages us to pursue pleasure. However, a closer look reveals some fascinating truth. In the original Greek, the word translated "lovely" is *prosphiles* (pronounced *prahs-fil-ACE*). This word occurs only this one time in the New Testament. Initially, I thought the uniqueness of this word would make it difficult for me to understand its precise meaning. I didn't know how I was going to build a framework for thinking about "whatever is lovely" around a word that is used only once in the entire New Testament.

Upon further investigation, I discovered that the word *prosphiles* is actually a combination of two fairly common Greek words: the word *pros* (pronounced *prahs*), which means "to, toward, or with," and the word *phileo* (pronounced *fil-EH-oh*), which is one of the four primary Greek words for "love." Once I recognized this, the meaning of *prosphiles*—the word we translate as "lovely"—became clear. The two root words together simply mean "toward love." Therefore, we are called to think in such a way as to move through our lives *toward* that which is *love*.

To be clear, this call isn't a license for us to move toward any kind of love of our choosing. This verse isn't describing a Valentine's Day type of love but specifically and exclusively a *phileo* kind of love. C. S. Lewis, in his work *The Four Loves*, lays out the four kinds of love from the Greek world: *agape*, *storge*, *eros*, and *phileo*. These four types of love shaped the world at that time, and they affect everyone who has read the New Testament.

1. *Agape* (pronounced *ahg-AH-pay*) is the unconditional, no-strings-attached kind of love that God expresses toward us.
2. *Storge* (pronounced *stor-GAY*) is an affection-oriented love, a brotherly love reserved for family and close friends.
3. *Eros* (pronounced *eh-RAHS*) is the romantic love upon which marriages are built.
4. *Phileo* is a friendship kind of love. It is a love based on affinity and shared likes and dislikes. As the *Theological Dictionary of the New Testament* describes, this love is "an affection based on personal attachment."[2]

Don't miss this: *phileo* is a love centered around personal pleasure. It is a love we give or receive based on what makes us glad, such as in a close friendship. We feel this love for something or someone precisely because they make us feel good. This love is not confined to human relationships in the Bible but is also associated with tangible things such as food, sleep, wine, knowledge—the things that give us pleasure.

Ancient Greeks used the word *phileo* in regard to the things they *liked* (they used *agape* for the things they *loved*), and these were the things that tended to be the foundation for pleasure. So the Philippians 4:8 directive to fix our thoughts on "whatever is lovely"—*prosphiles*—is telling us to have an attitude that moves us "toward love that brings pleasure," toward those things and people we love who make us glad and even happy.

The New Revised Standard Bible translates this passage as, "Whatever is pleasing . . . think about these things." While "lovely," used by the English Standard Version and most other translations, is probably more technically correct (because such versions translate the root *phileo* directly as a form of "love"), "pleasing" gets more to the idea of our having a mindset that moves us toward what makes us happy and gives us a profound sense of gratification and pleasure.

Let's be honest: we Christians don't tend to talk about our lives in this way. We usually leave pleasure to the hedonists in our culture, the celebrities who flaunt their pursuit of pleasure to the extent of decadence. Every generation has its poster children of decadence and hedonism. You probably don't have to think too long before some of the people who represent this approach to life come to mind. We Christians, on the other hand, tend to focus our thoughts on concepts such as sacrifice, surrender, faithfulness, devotion, and discipline. Though these things are certainly a large part of what it means to follow Jesus, we need to honor what Philippians 4:8 puts in front of us. We must not miss the Bible's call here to include the love of pleasure in our daily thoughts. Pleasure is one of the fuels that God uses to keep our lives going and growing. Whether we realize it or not, our lives are surrounded by pleasure and to some degree run on pleasure, and this isn't necessarily a bad thing.

Obviously, we must focus on a certain *kind* of pleasure. Otherwise, we might become more like the hedonists of our day than the Christlike followers of God we are called to be. Thinking about the "lovely things" is the mindset that moves us toward love. Three practical thoughts that flow from this biblical focus on *phileo* will guide our thoughts and direct our attention to the love that leads to pleasure.

Look for Pleasure in Legitimate Places

Earlier I wrote that the Bible uses *phileo* to describe love for things such as food, sleep, wine, and knowledge. We could easily interpret this to mean that the Bible legitimizes a strong affection for these and other things. However, a closer look at the context of how the Bible uses the word *phileo* in each of these instances reveals that sometimes such an interpretation is legitimate and sometimes it is not. Awareness of these contextual clues is helpful and instructive as we seek to understand how to have a proper relationship and experience legitimate pleasure with these things.

For example, consider food and its correlation to *phileo* love. In the Greek version of the Old Testament, Genesis 27 tells of the patriarch Isaac's desire to bless his son. He said to him, "Prepare for me delicious food, such as I love, and bring it to me so that I may eat, that my soul may bless you before I die" (v. 4). The delicious food is described using *phileo*. It is the food that he loves, that brings him pleasure. The use of this word here is a legitimate, God-ordained use of *phileo*. It is acceptable, even good, to find some pleasure in delicious food and the enjoyment of it.

Let's look at another example. God, through the prophet Hosea, said, "Even as the LORD loves [*agapeo*] the children of Israel, though they turn to other gods and love [*phileo*] cakes of raisins" (3:1). There's food again! Yet even a quick reading reveals that the tone is entirely different though the word used is the same. Why did God take a different tone in regard to this food? It's not because he doesn't like raisins!

Bible experts surmise that the reason God was against finding pleasure in these raisin cakes is because they could have been used in sacrifices to other gods (which makes sense, given the context of this verse).[3] These same experts point out that at this time cakes of raisins were a high-sugar delicacy from the Middle East. They were tempting and tasty. God was disappointed, then, that his people took too much pleasure in enjoying this tempting food and for all the wrong reasons. They found the wrong type of pleasure in enjoying it. Their love for this specific food had become a literal idol being sacrificed to false gods. This reminds me of a friend of mine who recently confessed that he loves his morning coffee so much that he thinks about it the night before as he goes to sleep. He admitted that his obsession was misplaced and over-the-top.

These two examples describe a legitimate love for food (in Isaac's case) and an illegitimate love for food (when it serves as an idol that begins to replace even God himself as our source of daily happiness). This surely resonates today. Our food-obsessed Christian subculture frowns on the sex-obsessed, alcohol-abusing, decadence-loving contemporary culture but has no problem with Christians who gorge themselves at the buffet after church without a thought or care in the world! We need a true Christlike mindset to distinguish between legitimate and illegitimate pleasure, even with something like food.

In following *phileo* throughout the Old Testament, we see additional warnings not to find too much pleasure in wine or sleep (see Prov. 21:17 and Isa. 56:10, respectively). Conversely, it's okay to find pleasure in wisdom and in family (see Prov. 29:3 and Gen. 37:4, respectively). In the New Testament, Jesus faulted the religious leaders of his day for finding pleasure in their places of honor, which caused the people in their communities to look at them and essentially say, "Boy, aren't they godly!" (see Matt. 23:1–12). But then he uplifted the pleasure found in loving friendships (such as with Lazarus, John, and Peter) (see John 11:36; 20:2; 21:15–17). The apostle Paul even applauded those who found pleasure in their church (Titus 3:15).

The point is clear: God offers us legitimate places to find pleasure, such as family, friends, wisdom, knowledge, understanding, and the church. At the same time, we are warned about illegitimate places to find pleasure, such as too much wine or too much sleep or the attraction, adoration, and applause of people. We can find *some* pleasure in things such as food, but we must be careful not to make an idol out of the object of this pleasure. The Bible plainly points to both legitimate and illegitimate places to search for pleasure.

Where do you look for pleasure? For many, the answer to this pointed question is expressed in the old Johnny Lee song in which he confessed, "I was looking for love in all the wrong places." We can all identify with that regret at times in our lives because of the tendency to settle for pleasure in the quest for love. Consequently, many of us are tempted to look for pleasure in the wrong things and pleasurable love in the wrong places.

As we apply this truly amazing call to think about the things and the people we love who bring us pleasure, we must remember that the search for pleasure must take place in legitimate places. Otherwise, we become just like the world around us—deep-seated in sin, finding pleasure in illegitimate places. Doing so may bring the sensation of pleasure in the moment, but in the long run it will harm our souls.

Nurture Healthy Sources of Pleasure

In addition to looking for pleasure in legitimate places, we are to nurture healthy sources of pleasure because it is the healthy sources of pleasure that provide the legitimate places of pleasure. This is the main point of Philippians 4:8 when it urges us to fix our thoughts on whatever is lovely: whatever is pleasurable in the realm of *phileo* love, nurture those sources. Like a sports car that runs well on high-octane gas but will quickly peter out on watered-down, low-octane fuel, we need to be fed daily from God's sources that will allow us to run our lives well. Here are a few sources that God graciously gives exactly for this purpose.

Safe People

Safe people as a source for daily pleasure truly are at the heart of the Bible's use of the word *phileo*. Though, as we

110

have seen, this word includes the love for pleasurable things such as food, sleep, wine, and knowledge, the vast majority of the uses of *phileo* in the Bible have to do with finding pleasure in "safe-harbor" friendships. These friendships are legitimate places of pleasure, and the safe people with whom we have these friendships are the healthy source of them. *Phileo* is the word used in the New Testament to describe Jesus's love for the apostle John as well as for Lazarus and Peter. Jesus found special joy and pleasure in his friendships with these three people. It's worth noting that the word *phileo* is even used to describe the love God the Father has for Jesus the Son, which shows us that the Trinity for all eternity finds relational pleasure within itself.

We can foster certain relationships that are built around this concept of *phileo*. These are safe relationships that are built upon shared values, affinity, and even similar experiences. They can be wonderful sources of life-giving joy.

As a pastor who lives a relatively public life, I've given a lot of thought to safe-harbor friendships. I live in a world in which many people I pastor consider me their friend. I'm honored by their esteem and consideration. But if we're being honest, we all have a limited capacity for the number of close friends we can enjoy in our lives. Consequently, over the years, I've had to use discernment regarding whom to let in to my full, private world. Obviously, this inner circle of friends includes my amazing wife, Kim. As I let others in, I developed a list of qualities and characteristics that describe trusted friends. Here is what my list looks like.

Honesty. I don't mean simple honesty. I mean the type of honesty that I call "red-dot honesty." This is a term I've adapted from my friend Larry Crabb, and it's based on the

red dot on a shopping mall map that tells you "you are here."
Red-dot honesty allows me to be transparently honest with
a trusted friend, to tell them exactly where I am and how
I'm doing, especially when how I'm doing isn't so good. It's
at times raw and unfiltered. Sometimes it's downright ugly.
Anyone in my inner circle needs to be able to hear my red-dot
honesty and to be red-dot honest with me too.

Candor. A friend can't be red-dot honest if they can't
speak with candor. We need to trust each other enough to
talk straight with each other without fluff and without feeling
the need to give a disclaimer of love every time we have to say
something tough to each other. In the same way, we don't need
to apologize any time we need to be candid and speak frankly,
because we're secure that our friendship is rooted in shared
trust and respect and can withstand candid conversation.

Acceptance. If we're going to be honest with each other,
we have to be able to accept each other and whatever we
share. Acceptance is not only assumed but also key to being
able to relate with each other candidly.

Shared values. I want to live a godly life and to increasingly
be the type of man God wants to shape me to be. My friends
need to share these values, and they need to have the integrity
to admit where they are in the pursuit of these shared values.
While I can be friends with people whose values are different
from my own, I can't realistically expect a person to speak
into my life with wisdom and understanding if their values
are drastically different from my own or if they are not living
with integrity regarding the values we share.

Humor. This one is huge for me. I wish more Christians
had a better sense of humor. Sometimes a lack of a sense of
humor keeps me from being a close friend to someone. We

need to be able to laugh with each other and sometimes at each other and ourselves. Some people are uncomfortable with this kind of humor. I'm not. For whatever reason, it puts me at ease with others. It makes my list of qualities I look for in a safe friendship.

Spiritual depth. I am a theologian. I love God. I think about God often throughout the day. I have come to appreciate friendships with others who have similarly determined to direct their thoughts toward God.

Self-knowledge. Knowing yourself is critical. I know the machinations of my soul. I know my motives, my strengths, and my weaknesses. The Eagles famously sang years ago, "Don't let the sound of your own wheels drive you crazy."[4] I don't think that's the problem of too many Christians. Most Christians aren't introspective enough. I am introspective. I need my trusted friends to be similarly introspective and to have a knowledge of themselves.

Others-centeredness. Nine times out of ten, the conversations I have with others are about the other person. While I don't need people continually asking me about my marriage and my kids and my world, I do enjoy conversations with friends that aren't about them. Safe-harbor friends understand the value of relational give-and-take, and this value is reflected in healthy conversations in which interest and concerns aren't one-sided.

Love of life as a gift from God to be thoroughly enjoyed. Even while having spiritual depth, my friends know how to relax and enjoy life. We have fun together. We play hard and then kick back together.

This is my list. Your list may look different. *Phileo* friendships are based on affinity and shared values and shared experiences. These are all key factors in how my list of qualities developed. These qualities serve as filters someone must "pass through" to become a trusted, safe-harbor friend. Please understand that I don't mean they have to pass a test. I mean that over time, I have come to identify these traits that I both value and strive to embody as valuable markers of my safe-harbor friendships.

Even while I count many people as friends, my roster of safe-harbor friends is much smaller. Some of them are back in Ohio, where I grew up. One is in London, Ontario, where I pastored for a few years. I have a few here in Scottsdale, Arizona, where I currently live. I can count them on one or two hands. They are trusted, they share values that matter to me, and they are a godly source of pleasure. These are safe-harbor friendships, built around *phileo*, and they each bring pleasure to my life.

To be certain, family members should be included as well. Though not all families are safe, the reality is that God designed the family to be a safe place. Husbands and wives should strive to have safe relationships. Parents should strive to make their homes safe places for their kids. To the extent that we can do so, we should strive to make our extended families safe places too. Safe people are the most vital source of pleasure; as such, they are the first source we should nurture.

Solid Activities

By "solid," I simply mean activities that are of good, substantial quality rather than unhealthy and hollow with regard to bringing pleasure into our lives. I can't mention all such activities. I only remind you to allow the Bible as well as trusted, godly people to guide you in determining what is solid when it comes to "whatever is lovely" for you.

Two men who are friends of mine have an amazing story about exchanging activities that were hollow for ones that are solid. Denny started drinking alcohol when he was eighteen years old. He quickly developed a reputation for doing outrageous things whenever he became intoxicated. Rich, likewise, started drinking as a teenager. As an adult, and even after becoming a Christian, he was an everyday drinker who increasingly made excuses to avoid being anywhere he couldn't have a drink in his hand by five o'clock. As both Denny and Rich continued drinking to excess, they built up protective walls around themselves. These walls created barriers between themselves and God and between themselves and others. Though they functioned well in polite society, inwardly they knew something was not right.

Rich eventually came to a breaking point. He reached out to a Christian friend who led him into recovery. As Rich pursued restoration through recovery, he determined that he needed to be honest with his friend Denny, admitting to him that he was an alcoholic. He told Denny that he'd have to miss Bible study because he needed to attend a recovery group scheduled that same night. Denny said, "Right away I teared up because I recognized that God was using Rich to reach out to me. Through Rich, God was saying, 'Denny, it's time.' And so I immediately asked Rich if I could join him in his recovery program."

Rich said that Denny's vulnerability impacted him in a significant way. "When Denny was open and honest with me, the relief was overpowering," he said. "Today my children are so relieved that they have their dad back and a grandfather for their children. They feel like they have a whole new guy on their hands, and they do."

Denny changed as well. "Now having been sober for more than three years, my life is filled with much more joy. Rich and I have started a group for men who are in recovery, whether for alcohol or a drug issue. We find so much joy helping men in their sobriety," he said.

Denny and Rich's story shows both the value and the power of finding pleasure in solid activities. God showed each of them, using the other, that the misuse of alcohol was not a good, substantial activity for their lives. It was hollow. We are all well served to take an inventory of our own activities and to ask not only if they give us pleasure but also if they are good for us. If at the end of that assessment we have a God-given sense that an activity is hollow and/or hurtful, we need to take action to exchange it for an activity that is solid because it is godly.

Again, I don't have a master list of what those activities are, but I have never gone wrong when I have followed the Bible's teaching when it comes to right and wrong. I have also never lost out by following the advice of people in my life who know God. The two things I ask myself whenever I'm not sure whether an activity is solid are "What does the Bible say about this?" and "What would Kim or one of my safe-harbor friends say about this?"

This is not to say I have never made bad choices. When I have, often I failed to heed God's Word or the wise counsel of the godly people around me. For instance, there have been plenty of times over the years when I thought a certain financial purchase would give me pleasure. Usually, it was a car-related purchase. Sometimes my wife reminded me that it was not a good time for us to make such a purchase. She has almost always been right in these (and other) conversations, and I have done well to listen, even when it meant delayed gratification. There were other times I didn't listen to her and later realized I had made an unwise purchase. I hate eating crow. And just so we're clear: my wife is not a killjoy. Not at all. In fact, she loves that I find pleasure in certain tangible areas of my life (as well as in her and in our family), and she is all for it. At the same time, she is wise. I have never gone wrong listening to that kind of wisdom. Part of learning to nurture healthy sources of pleasure involves allowing the Bible and godly people to become wonderful guardrails for us, to ensure that our pleasure is rightly founded and consistently solid.

A Sound View of God

God is the God of profound relationality. Sadly, so many Christians miss this. I'm always disappointed to hear Christians describe their relationship with God as an "it." I'll ask a question like, "How would you describe your experience with God?" to which they'll reply, "Well, I was raised with *it*" or "When I was in high school and college, I fell away from *it*" or "I came back to *it*, and now I'm doing really well with *it*." Too many Christians refer to their relationship as an "it" because they've reduced Christianity to a lifestyle. They've reduced their faith to a set of doctrines they believe. They've reduced their experience to a worldview that guides them in a general direction. And while none of this is bad on its own, *it* misses the point that we are in a love relationship with a *him*! God is Father, Son, and Holy Spirit.

117

The bottom line is that this love relationship with God that you and I have matters most. We are hardwired to pursue delight, and when we don't experience that delight by being in a healthy relationship with God, we will invariably seek pleasure elsewhere. If you never cultivate your spiritual life as a healthy source of pleasure, love, and joy, you are an accident waiting to happen. Without a healthy spiritual life, you will, by necessity, look for pleasure in all the wrong places. Sadly, many people do exactly that every day. Having a healthy view of God all boils down to "it" versus "him."

This is why I spend so much time as a pastor talking about things like truth and right doctrine, the relationality and grace of God, prayer as a lifestyle, Bible study, participation in a small group environment, serving others, and even regular personal time spent with God (commonly referred to as "quiet time" in Christian terminology). We don't do these things simply to show our devotion, sacrifice, and discipline. We do these things because they can become sources of pleasure in our walk with God. These things help us foster more of "him" and less of "it." The more we practice these things, the more we train our souls to delight in God himself. God desires and longs for us to be in a right relationship with him through Jesus Christ, even to the point that we find our sufficiency and satisfaction and joy in him and our relationship with him. The renowned pastor and author John Piper calls this "Christian Hedonism," or learning to find our utmost pleasure in God himself.[5]

Always Remember to Give More Than You Get

A third point concerns this idea of pleasure: let us never forget that when it comes to pleasure, we need to give more than we get. This is so simple but so profound. Jesus taught us this idea and demonstrated it consistently. He continually brought pleasure to the people in his company. In the book of Acts, when the apostle Paul was on the shore of Ephesus saying good-bye to the church there, he quoted Jesus in his parting words, saying, "In all things I have shown you that by working hard in this way we must help the weak and remember the words of the Lord Jesus, how he himself said, 'It is more blessed to give than to receive'" (20:35). This word *blessed* literally means "to make happy," and it conveys the same idea behind *phileo* love leading to pleasure and joy. From this meaning, we can understand that a key part of our happiness is found when we stop seeking pleasure for pleasure's sake and focus on others. When we learn to give rather than get, we find the most pleasure.

A family in our church not long ago experienced the pain of the death of their child. Walking with them has been a bittersweet experience. Understandably, their grief and sadness have been profound. There is no way to take away the constant ache in their souls. One of the things they have found, however, is that even in the first year of their grief, they have been able to be used by God to minister to other people who have experienced a similar loss. As they have focused not just on themselves in their loss but also on others who have experienced similar tragedies, they have found pleasure in helping others. God has used even this painful experience in their lives to bring them pleasure. He has done this through their willingness to give more than they have received.

This family has modeled for me the importance of others-centered giving. Give time. Give care. Give attention. Give a listening ear. Give sacrificial service. Give resources. As we develop a way of thinking that focuses on "whatever is lovely," we need to remember that pleasure is found most profoundly through giving rather than getting.

Don't ever let anyone tell you that Christians do not find pleasure in life. We do! We just have a different take on pleasure and how to pursue it. Focusing on "whatever is lovely" means we look for pleasure in legitimate places, nurture healthy sources of pleasure, and always strive to give more of it than we get.

7

YOUR LIFE
ON A BILLBOARD

Where Who You Are Meets What Others See

Live so that you wouldn't be ashamed to sell the family parrot to the town gossip.

Will Rogers

Most people are familiar with the name John Grisham. He is the award-winning author of more than thirty-five novels, and over 275 million copies of his books have sold worldwide. His writings have been translated into more than forty languages.[1] Several of his books have been made into blockbuster movies starring A-list celebrities. However, before he was "famous author John Grisham," he was "struggling-to-be-discovered author John Grisham."

121

In the 1980s, Grisham was a Mississippi state legislator with a passion for writing. He wrote the manuscript for *A Time to Kill* and submitted it to publishing houses and agents. In all, twenty-eight publishers rejected the book before a small publisher picked it up for a modest print run of five thousand copies. A year later the book was published with little fanfare. Grisham purchased one thousand copies of the book himself and toured the southeast United States to sell them.[2]

While this all unfolded, Grisham wrote his second novel, *The Firm*. A major publisher picked up the book, and it remained atop the bestseller list for forty-seven weeks. With success, publishing houses came to him. In the time since, Grisham has enjoyed a long-standing relationship with a major publisher, with books spanning multiple genres. His widespread success has allowed him to parlay his name recognition to advocate for social causes that matter to him. His longtime publisher eventually bought the rights to his first novel, *A Time to Kill*—the one with an initial print run of five thousand copies—and republished it. To date, it has sold more than twenty million copies! Grisham's reputation had now preceded him.

"Whatever Is Commendable"

As John Grisham's experience illustrates, reputation is a powerful thing. Unfortunately, many of us give little thought to our reputation as we go through life on a day-to-day basis. Yet the Bible tells us to do exactly that. Our sixth way of thinking is stated, "Whatever is commendable . . . think about these things" (Phil. 4:8). The New American Standard

Bible says, "Whatever is of good repute . . . dwell on these things." Even more pointedly, the King James Version states, "Whatsoever things are of good report . . . think on these things." The terms "commendable," "good repute," and "things of good report" are all translated from the Greek word *euphemos* (pronounced *EU-fay-mahs*), written in the original biblical text two thousand years ago.

Euphemos is made up of two rather common, straightforward Greek words. The first is the word *eu* (pronounced *you*), which means "good or well." The second is the word *pheme* (pronounced *FAY-may*), which means "report; news or fame." The word *pheme* is used when Jesus returned from being tempted in the desert for forty days and nights. Scripture reads, "And Jesus returned in the power of the Spirit to Galilee, and a report [*pheme*] about him went out through all the surrounding country. And he taught in their synagogues, being glorified by all" (Luke 4:14–15). News spread about Jesus; people were talking, and a reputation had been established.

The word *euphemos*, therefore, literally means "good report" or "good fame." When others look at you and your life, they say good things about you. The importance of this needs to become entrenched in our thinking. According to Philippians 4:8, we are supposed to consider and contemplate our reputation—what others are saying—for it becomes a part of our overall view of ourselves before almighty God.

The Reputation Equation

A rather potent equation makes up a reputation:

our behavior + others' assessments = reputation

A reputation is made up of the things we say and do combined with others' observations, assessments, comments, and conversations about what we say and do. Only when our behavior and others' assessments of it converge do we have a reputation.

To illustrate, if I have a justice-oriented mindset, I am focused on righting wrongs (bringing justice to the world) and acting on my convictions. Hopefully, other people will observe my words and my deeds and as a result will think or even say, "Wow, Jamie is truly a man who loves the downtrodden and is willing to do something about all the injustice around us!" Because of my behavior and others' assessments of it, I will have developed a reputation that is good and honorable, at least by the standards of a community that values justice. Unfortunately, it's also possible that someone can see my behavior, assess it unfairly, and judge it unfavorably!

The following chart shows how the two components can combine to result in different kinds of reputations:

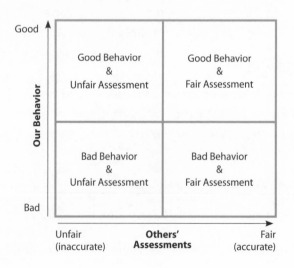

This chart explains why you can have a good or bad reputation, or even a fair or unfair reputation. You see, your reputation comes down to the same components that make up every reputation: your behavior and others' assessments. The good report of Philippians 4:8 is represented by the upper right quadrant. When our behavior is good and the assessment of others regarding our good behavior is fair and accurate, a "good report" (*euphemos*) is the result. That's where our focus should be. We always need to keep our reputation in our thoughts so that we strive to have a "good report."

Reputations are tricky though. We can't always control how other people will assess our behavior. There may be times when we have good behavior, but other people don't see it as good or agree that it is godly. Their assessment is unfair or inaccurate, resulting in an unfairly assessed, bad reputation, as shown in the upper left quadrant. The Bible speaks to these types of circumstances, which are identified by the word *slander*. The apostle Paul wrote about it, stating, "We put no obstacle in anyone's way, so that no fault may be found with our ministry, but as servants of God we commend ourselves in every way: . . . through honor and dishonor, through slander and praise. We are treated as impostors, and yet are true" (2 Cor. 6:3–4, 8).

The use of these two terms, *slander* and *praise*, in 2 Corinthians 6:8 is both interesting and relevant in the context of reputation. The Greek word for "praise" is a variation of *euphemos*, expressing the sentiment of a "good report" in the form of praise. However, the Greek word for "slander" is *dusphemia* (pronounced *doos-fay-MEE-ah*), which is made up of the roots *dus* and *phemia*. We know that *pheme* means "report," but whereas *eu* means "good," *dus* means "hard, difficult, or grievous." Therefore, *dusphemia* is a "grievous report" or, in today's language, "slander."

Obviously, the only aspect that we can directly control regarding our reputation is our behavior. Slander is so grievous for many of us because we have learned that there are times in this fallen world when we do good but others misunderstand it, don't appreciate it, or even don't see it as good. Their unfair assessment of our good deeds is reported inaccurately. When this happens, it hurts. The apostle Paul certainly identified with this challenge, as shown in 2 Corinthians 6:8. When his good labors were fairly and accurately assessed, praise resulted. However, when his good labors were unfairly or inaccurately assessed, the result was slander.

When people slander us, they say unfair things about us. This happens to everyone. As a pastor of a good-sized church that does lots of ministry and engages with our culture, I receive both praise and slander. When things are going well and our efforts are well received, I am often graced to be the one who receives the praise. At the same time, though, when our efforts are inaccurately or unfairly assessed, I am often the object of the resulting slander.

We all experience times when our reputation is threatened, not because our behavior is inconsistent or bad but because others' assessments aren't always accurate or fair. We may try to help others see that our behavior is well-intentioned and even good, but other people don't always see it that way. We learn, often through unfortunate experiences, that we can't directly control others' assessments of our behavior.

In the bottom right quadrant, we see that when our behavior is bad and others' assessments of it are fair, the result is fairly assessed, bad reputation. Philippians 4:8 calls us to keep our thoughts on our reputation so that we don't become a lower-right-quadrant Christian who is marked by a well-deserved, bad reputation.

The lower left quadrant represents bad behavior that others inaccurately call good. Hopefully, this description isn't characteristic of you or anyone in your Christian world. It is, however, all too common in the world around us. People often behave decadently or in an ungodly way only to be praised and celebrated by the world for doing so. This "antihero" behavior is the stuff of a lower-left-quadrant reputation. Shock jocks on the radio know all too well this lower left quadrant.

As we can see, both behavior and others' assessments of that behavior help form a reputation. We have little to no control over how other people assess our words, attitudes, and actions. At the same time, we certainly can control our own behavior. This is precisely the point of Philippians 4:8. "Whatever is commendable" includes whatever is good that other people might, when they are thinking rightly, see for what it is and commend or report well about. These commendation-worthy things must be a part of our daily mindset.

When we are thinking about "whatever is commendable," we are "thinking reputation." To be clear, though, when we are "thinking reputation," we are not thinking about ways to please other people. We have already established that we can't directly control others' assessments. We can, however, keep the idea of a good reputation in our thoughts so that we strive to have a level of goodness in our lives as followers of Jesus that just might turn the heads of those around us, resulting in a good reputation.

The Building Blocks of a Good Reputation

As we strive to build a good reputation based on good behavior, we need to determine what good behavior entails. What can we do that others will see as good and godly in our lives? What should we focus on in our lives that just might result in a "commendable" reputation?

These are important questions. Don't overlook them. The way the average Christian answers these questions has concerned me for years. By the way most Christians behave today, we might infer that the things they believe amount to a commendable reputation are

- rigid morality
- spot-on doctrine
- conservative views
- church attendance

These are the things Christians tend to tout to the onlooking world. These are the things many Christians present to others in their efforts to put their best foot forward. Many Christians believe these things will give them a commendable reputation with their neighbors, friends, coworkers, and service providers.

However, as good as these things might be (and they are all reasonably or arguably good), the Bible offers a much different list as it guides us to build a good reputation. Tracking how the New Testament uses the word *eu*—the first half of the word *euphemos*—reveals to us what the Bible sees as "good." The word *eu* is used alone four times in the New Testament, and these four uses reveal four kinds of behavior that serve as the true building blocks of a good reputation:

- faithfulness
- kindness
- righteousness
- honor

Let's look more closely at each of these four behaviors.

Faithfulness

Jesus used a parable to teach that every one of his followers has been given various spiritual gifts and natural talents to be put to use. He taught that people are differently gifted and variably talented (for example, some people have one talent, others two, and still others five). The key is not how many gifts we have received but what we do with them. Notice what the master in Jesus's parable says to the two servants who were faithful in maximizing the blessings provided to them:

> His master said to him, "Well done, good and faithful servant. You have been faithful over a little; I will set you over much. Enter into the joy of your master." . . . His master said to him, "Well done, good and faithful servant. You have been faithful over a little; I will set you over much. Enter into the joy of your master." (Matt. 25:21, 23)

The master commended both of them, saying, "Well done!" Notice the repetition. Jesus clearly used this repeated language to emphasize his point. To commend the faithful workers, the master used the word *eu* to describe them as good. Here faithfulness before God and others is equated with good. "Well done" is the kind of good God uses as a building block for a commendable reputation.

The fact that faithfulness is a building block for a good reputation only makes sense. Most people in this world long for faithfulness and consistency, and they sure don't mind when they see it and experience it. In a world in which many marriages end in divorce (often due to unfaithfulness), most people are touched and moved when they see someone steward a marriage faithfully over twenty, thirty, forty, fifty, even sixty years! Faithfulness builds a good reputation.

In a world in which people are knocked off center in their belief in and trust of God when bad things happen, they are inspired and moved and even confounded when they see someone remain faithful to God in the midst of difficult times and troubling circumstances. Faithfulness builds a good reputation.

In a world in which it's hard to find a faithful friend—someone who will stick with you through thick and thin no matter what—people will be blown away when they find that kind of faithfulness. Faithfulness builds a good reputation.

Truly, the first building block of a biblical *euphemos* (a good report) is faithfulness. When we think about our reputation, we should think about faithfulness.

Kindness

The Bible captures a moment when Jesus was being harassed because he had allowed a woman to pour an expensive bottle of perfume on him, which was an honorable thing to do in that culture at that time. The onlookers argued that the perfume could have been sold and the profits used to feed the poor. The Bible says that the people were indignant over the woman's decision to anoint Jesus. In the midst of responding to the crowd, Jesus said, "For you always have the poor with you, and whenever you want, you can do good for them" (Mark 14:7).

Jesus's statement "you can do good" (another instance of the Greek word *eu*) is often misunderstood. Most people who read this maintain that Jesus meant the disadvantaged and poor will always be with us. Poverty and injustice are part and parcel of a fallen world's existence. Hence, they argue, there are more important and immediate things we can focus on, which is what the woman did in pouring perfume on Jesus. Such people use Jesus's words here to actually diminish doing good to those in need. But this interpretation misses Jesus's plain point. Though he was defending the woman who poured perfume on him, Jesus was also making clear that it is good to minister to the poor and those in need. He was not diminishing this call to do good to those in need—not at all. He was saying that, whenever we want, we have the resources and the ability to do good for them. And this is a good thing. Kindness in the form of helping those in need is clearly linked by Jesus to the kind of good that forms a commendable reputation.

Christians are sometimes easy targets for misplaced criticism. The common tactic is to point out the "dark spots" in Christianity's two-thousand-year history, when the deeds of people who self-identified as Christians clearly contradicted the ethic and ways of Jesus, such as the Crusades. While we need to be humble and own these lowlights, we can also point out that these are the rare exception in Christian history. The more common standard has been much more honorable and admirable.

For more than two thousand years now, Christians have led the way in caring for those in need. Even amid some of our darkest spots in history, this consistent effort of care has given us a "salt and light" reputation in a world that is not our home. In every age, whether it has been the early church, the Middle Ages, the Renaissance, the Enlightenment, the Industrial Revolution, the Technological Revolution, and now the Digital Revolution, Christians have prioritized kindness and justice and caring for people in need.

Henry Ford once said, "You can't build a reputation on what you are going to do, but only as to what you have done in the form of accomplishment."[3] From medical missions to inner-city soup kitchens to Third-World relief efforts (such as World Vision, Compassion International, and Samaritan's Purse, among many others) to orphanages in places such as India, Mexico, and Haiti to shelters for those who have no homes, Christians have an amazing track record in leading the way when it comes to caring for the poor and disenfranchised.

People don't necessarily see the solid doctrine we embrace. They don't necessarily agree with our reasonable, cogent politics. They aren't necessarily impressed by our consistent attendance at or involvement in our church. They might completely misunderstand the motives behind our morality. But when an onlooking world observes and assesses our kindness, it becomes knit deeply and wonderfully into our reputation. Others may even see our actions and respond to our kindness. When we think about our reputation, we should think about kindness.

Righteousness

The book of Acts shares a third use of the Greek word *eu*, when the Jerusalem leaders gave instructions to Paul and

Barnabas for how to deal with a particular Jewish-Gentile controversy occurring at the church in Antioch. In determining whether Gentiles had to obey all the Old Testament Jewish religious laws to show they were followers of Jesus, the leaders said:

> For it has seemed good to the Holy Spirit and to us to lay on you no greater burden than these requirements: that you abstain from what has been sacrificed to idols, and from blood, and from what has been strangled, and from sexual immorality. If you keep yourselves from these, you will do well. (Acts 15:28–29)

This passage obviously addresses a first-century conflict and the kind of righteousness based on Old Testament laws and values that would build unity among Jewish and Gentile forms of Christianity. Even so, the point still stands that there is a link here between a certain level of righteousness and "doing well" (*eu*) that creates a commendable reputation.

Following God and obeying his Word—though at times grating on a fallen and decadent world—still have the powerful potential of making others look at us and at the very least say, "They sure do walk the walk and live out what they claim to believe!" We don't want to come across as holier than thou, to be sure. However, consider the alternative. If we don't have a level of righteousness and morality, we will be labeled hypocrites. We don't claim to be perfect, and everyone struggles with hypocrisy to some degree, but as people who claim to be filled with the Holy Spirit and to be followers of Jesus Christ, we should have a measure of righteousness that is distinctively different from the standards of the world in which we live. We should also remember that righteousness takes a lifetime to build up, and it can be lost in a moment. It is precious, and even the unbelieving world seems to agree that it sets Christians apart in terms of reputation.

Aspects of righteousness such as integrity, morality, and character are usually admired (especially when combined with humility and grace), and therefore righteousness truly is a building block of a good reputation. When we think about our reputation, we should think about righteousness.

Honor

Through the apostle Paul in the book of Ephesians, God issues a command to children with a promise attached to it, declaring, "Honor your father and mother . . . that it may go well with you and that you may live long in the land" (6:2–3).

Here the word *honor* means "to show respect; to value; to revere."[4] Honoring our parents doesn't mean we always must agree with them, but we do have to show them respect, even in the midst of carving out our own life and faith, even if and when we disagree with them. Honoring someone has more to do with how we say something than what we say. Honorable people speak truth. They just do so, as Scripture says, "with gentleness and respect" (1 Pet. 3:15). When we behave in this way, our honor is noticed not only by our parents but also by others who see us in action. This is what the verse means when it says that it "may go well" with you. This is the Greek word *eu* again, connoting that when we show honor, there is good attached to it, good that benefits our reputation.

This idea of honor enhancing our reputation does not stop with just our parents. We are supposed to honor our spouse.

We are supposed to honor our boss and employer. We are even supposed to honor our pastor (I like that one!). We are supposed to show honor in all our relationships. God understands how important showing honor is in developing a good reputation. When we think about our reputation, we should think about honor.

Reputation Matters

As I am writing the final words to this chapter, I am hiding away at a little house my wife and I have in Northern Michigan. It's our retreat place. Quiet and peaceful, it's away from all the distractions that consume our mental energies back in the Southwest. The town this house is in has a population that is one-seventh the population of my church.

Today the air conditioner gave out in our little house. Not a good thing given the humid Midwest summer days. I called the HVAC guy in the small town in which our little house is nestled. My neighbor told me when we first came here that not only is this guy good at what he does but he is also one "stand-up guy." Not a bad endorsement in a small town in which everybody knows everybody. When I asked my neighbor why he felt this way about the man, he said, "He is just a supernice guy. He doesn't hassle anyone, and he never overcharges. He's honest and dependable."

As I have gotten to know this man, his reputation has proven true. He has an obvious love for people and a gentle demeanor and seems to know his stuff when it comes to HVAC. And wouldn't you know, he's a sold-out follower of Jesus. What a vital combination, a powerful witness for the Lord.

Our reputation is the combination of our behavior and others' assessments. We can't control those assessments, but we can control our behavior. Let's dream about all the various whatevers we can pursue throughout the day as our behavior is marked by faithfulness, kindness, righteousness, and honor. When our thoughts are focused on these building blocks, we create the right environment in which a good reputation can develop. A good reputation is something that pleases God and is certainly something he can use.

8

A NEW KIND
OF AWESOME

Linking Excellence to the Things That Matter

"If there is any excellence . . ."

Christ says, "Give Me all. I don't want so much of your time and so much of your money and so much of your work: I want you. . . . No half-measures are any good."

C. S. Lewis

If there is one thing that Americans love, it's excellence. We want excellent clothes, excellent food, excellent education, excellent cars, excellent sports teams, excellent customer service, excellent government (no comment), excellent internet service, excellent health care, and an excellent retirement package. In our modern age, in which a level of excellence is within reach on so many levels, most of us expect excellence in our lives.

In fact, when we have a less-than-excellent experience, we make it known. A 2015 study done by the *Consumer Reports* National Research Center found that nearly 90 percent of Americans had dealt with customer service in some way during the past year. Of those surveyed, more than half reported leaving a store without making their intended purchase due to poor customer service. A whopping 57 percent hung up the phone on a customer service representative due to a failed resolution.[1] The results are in: Americans love the good life, and anything less than excellence will not do.

"If There Is Any Excellence"

We might find it strange, then, to hear the Bible say, "*If* there is any excellence." Our response might be, "If? What do you mean *if*? Of course there is excellence in life. The Bible almost seems to suggest that excellence is a rare commodity." It is, at least as far as the right kind of excellence is concerned. God's kind of excellence.

The Greek word translated as "excellence" in Philippians 4:8 is *arete* (pronounced *ar-eh-TAY*), and it also means "outstanding goodness."[2] When this word was penned two thousand years ago, in the middle of the vast and powerful Greco-Roman Empire, it was a common word among the Greeks and Romans but a word that was rarely used by the writers of the Bible.

The Greeks loved this word. In their culture, they used this word regularly to describe the mastery of a specific field or a person with a particular personal endowment, the idea being that excellence was measured by achievement in specific areas of life. For the Greeks, everything from land to animals to parts of the body could be measured by the yardstick of excellence.[3]

In the time of Homer, *arete* was used to describe manliness—the excellence of men in military and battle settings. Greek philosophers likewise used this word to describe intellectual prowess and virtue. The Greeks also used this word to refer to the gods, associating their power with excellence.[4] There was even a minor Greek deity named *Arete*, and she was the goddess of goodness, virtue, and valor.[5]

From 1980 to 2001, the US Army had a slogan most Americans will remember: "Be all you can be." It was our military's way of drawing young men and women into a life of military service—enticing them with a call to personal excellence. The Greeks thought similarly about life. From war to education to athletics to commerce, the name of the game was excellence. *Arete* described the difference between a life of mediocrity and a life of success.

This is not too dissimilar from our contemporary culture. As already noted, we too strive after excellence in just about every endeavor in life. We too see excellence as the pinnacle of human achievement. We too attain excellence through the application of human ingenuity. Like the ancient Greeks, we have knit this idea of "outstanding goodness" richly into the fabric of our society. The late Steve Jobs captured this sentiment, saying, "We don't get a chance to do that many things, and everyone should be really excellent. Because this is our life."[6]

And why not? How could excellence ever not be a good thing?

From a Waterfall to a Trickle

When the writers of the Bible encountered this Greek word, their response was somewhat unexpected. Whereas the Greeks used this word hundreds of times in all kinds of settings and applications, the biblical writers did so only sparsely and with great care. Their usage was like the difference between a waterfall and a trickle.

In the Greek version of the Old Testament, *arete* appears only a half dozen times. In the New Testament, it appears even less. We must ask, What would cause such a drought? In a culture that utilized the word *excellence* consistently and regularly, why pull back the throttle so drastically? It's not like *arete* is a swear word or a vulgar term. Certainly, the Bible avoids these. So why the trickle, especially with a word as positive and as uplifting as *excellence*?

The difference in usage comes down to worldview. It boils down to how one *thinks* about the world around them. Look at how the *Theological Dictionary of the New Testament* answers our query:

> To understand the few passages where *aretê* is used in the NT it is important that the [Greek version of the Old Testament] applies the Greek concept of virtue in a distinctive way. . . . For a [biblical] world in which man constantly saw himself morally responsible before a holy God the Greek concept of virtue [excellence] could not finally fulfill its apparent promise. Though not irreligious, it was far too anthropocentric and this-worldly in orientation. What both the OT and NT attest is not human achievements or merits but the acts of God.[7]

Simply put, the biblical writers were leery of championing human success attained through human power. They were more concerned with the excellence of God himself as well as the resultant kind of excellence we can achieve when we think and act according to his ways. God says that any attempt at excellence without his direction and his empowering might, like a beautiful car with an underpowered engine, look good on the outside but won't get us very far due to what's on the inside. Only his take on what is excellent, combined with his energy fueling us, will suffice. Anything else is, at best, paltry and, at worst, dangerous.

As a result of this perspective, the Old Testament writers used the word *arete* a mere six times, with five of them describing God himself and one describing a godly high priest (see Zech. 6:13). In the New Testament, *arete* appears in only four verses, twice to refer to God and twice to refer to Christians who follow God and tap into his view of what is excellent. This is a vastly different approach to the word and the concept of excellence. In both volume and substance, the Bible's take on excellence differs significantly from that of the prevailing culture—whether it be ancient Greece or modern America.

In sum, then, the Bible's view of excellence involves two key components.

1. Any pursuit of excellence must be *biblically guided* in both choice and direction.
2. Any application of excellence must be *Spirit empowered* in both motivation and action.

In other words, as people who want to be intentional in the way we think, we must approach excellence by allowing the Bible to guide us in what to be excellent in and allowing the Holy Spirit to empower our excellence as we live a God-dependent life. Only as we fuel our pursuits of excellence with these dual components can we sufficiently live out the call of Philippians 4:8 to "think excellence." Only with these two driving qualifiers can we begin to understand why the call is to determine *"if* there is any excellence."

The Men from the Boys and the Women from the Girls

Excellence that is biblically guided and Spirit empowered may seem like such a simple idea, but let's not rush past it. Our pursuits of excellence, guided by what the Bible says and empowered by God's indwelling Holy Spirit, are foundational to what it means to follow God in this fallen world. Pursuing excellence using these concepts is what, as the old saying goes, "separates the men from the boys and the women from the girls" in the Christian life. It is the dividing line between those who dabble in their faith and those who are all in. It's the difference between toddlers who still drink milk from a sippy cup and mature adults who eat filet mignon and russet potatoes (see Heb. 5:12–14).

I want you to think of the opposite of biblically guided and Spirit-empowered excellence. It is culturally guided and self-empowered. It is pursued by those who go with the flow of the world around them, getting their cues from daytime talk shows, *New York Times* bestsellers, barroom conversations, major news outlets, and/or whatever their own finite minds might think is right and good. The tone and direction of such excellence are set by the prevailing mood of society at large:

- excellence in having the right marriage partner, even if it means ditching the one you have
- excellence in amassing more wealth, which breeds security, even if it means forgoing generosity and sacrificial giving
- excellence in vocational achievement, even if it means cutting corners to get ahead
- excellence in emotional happiness, even if it means damaging personal relationships and not having to forgive

Approached this way, excellence is culturally guided.

Once we adopt our culture's pursuit of excellence, we easily take the next step to fuel this pursuit by self-empowerment. *We* pursue our goals. *We* make things happen. *We* muster up all the internal energy we can to drive ourselves toward our culturally guided goals. Every day becomes a slugfest to get ahead and to get the most out of life this side of heaven. And if we get stuck, we find a solution. We read some self-help books. We go to therapy. We watch an inspirational movie. We dig deep into ourselves to find the discipline and the reserves to forge ahead. Self-empowerment is the name of the game.

The two approaches to excellence reveal the age-old battle between what the Bible calls the "flesh" and the "Spirit" (see Gal. 5:16–25). The difference is between relying on our human, fleshly strength to get ahead and relying on God's Spirit to guide us and empower us in our pursuits. Are we going to approach our pursuits of excellence with a culturally guided, self-empowered mindset or a biblically guided, Spirit-empowered one? Are we going to live what the King

James Bible calls a "carnal" life (1 Cor. 3:3), or are we going to live a life in which we are sold out to the things of God in the way we think, feel, and act? There is a lot at stake in this pursuit of excellence, both in what we pursue and in how we pursue it.

When Jesus walked this earth, he modeled for us what it looks like to live a God-dependent, God-obsessed, God-fueled life. He said that "man shall not live by bread alone, but by every word that comes from the mouth of God" (Matt. 4:4). He clearly pointed toward biblically guided excellence. He revealed that his empowerment came directly from faith in the Father, saying, "Truly, truly, I say to you, the Son can do nothing of his own accord, but only what he sees the Father doing. . . . I and the Father are one" (John 5:19; 10:30). Every pursuit of excellence that Jesus made was guided by God's revelation in his Word and fueled by the Holy Spirit through regular connection with the Father. As a result, Jesus lived an excellent life. He lived a perfect life, sinless in all he did. And though you and I cannot possibly reach perfection in this life, we can pursue excellence patterned after Jesus. Biblically guided, Spirit-empowered excellence worked for him. It's bound to work for us.

Excellence in the Marketplace

A friend of mine is a career stockbroker who has been in the business for more than thirty years. He is good at what he does and has provided well for his family over the years. He originally worked for a couple of reputable firms and now runs his own investment sales and advisory practice. The only things he has ever known are trading stocks and making investments. These activities are what he will be doing until he retires or dies. To use the language of this chapter, he is "excellent" at what he does.

He is also a strong Christian. He came to faith in Christ as a young adult. Over the years, he has developed a consistent walk with the Lord through a regular devotional life that includes personal Bible study and prayer. He and his wife are involved in their church. They have passed on their faith to their now adult children. They give their time, talents, and treasures generously to God in all they do.

As I have journeyed with my friend over the years, I have been amazed at the progression he has made in his understanding and application of what vocational excellence means for him as a Christian. Very early on, right after he came to faith in the late 1980s, he began to wrestle with what may be called the "seedy" nature of the financial industry. Surrounded by the amassing of personal and corporate wealth, he saw how easy it was to allow greed to take over and become the driving force in this industry. He observed that when greed runs the show, it's only a matter of time until integrity becomes threatened. He experienced a lot of pressure to get clients to move their money around to different investment vehicles, as the commission for the broker was tied to such action. Many days my friend would leave the office feeling "dirty," simply because of the nature of the work he had to do.

As conviction set in, he did all the things one might expect a man of integrity to do. He began monitoring much more closely his motives for encouraging his clients to invest in new or different financial vehicles. He challenged the norms and began asking himself difficult questions. Were his actions truly in the client's best interest? Or were his decisions driven by the commission? Or maybe a combination of both? What was driving the advice being given, flesh or Spirit?

He also developed a worldview that put money and materialism in their proper place. He began to realize, as C. S. Lewis posited, the difference between "first things" and "second things."[8] First things are the things of God, his values and his priorities. Faith, hope, and love are included in first things. Second things are still good things, but they are never to have first-place status. Money, possessions, hobbies, physical fitness, and nice vacations are examples of second things. This distinction helped my friend to stay focused throughout the day on what matters most.

As my friend grew in his understanding of what it means to be biblically guided and Spirit empowered at work, he did something that blew my mind. One day he shared with me that though he was diligently applying his new biblical worldview of first and second things combined with his Spirit-enabled check on his motives, he still felt surrounded by a culture of greed throughout the day. To combat this, he began each day by envisioning an invisible bubble around his body—a bubble impermeable by the world around him. Only he and Jesus existed in this bubble. As he went throughout the day, he pictured the Lord with him. Sometimes he talked with the Lord. Other times he simply existed in calm peace and joy, knowing that God was with him. Though some might think this rather strange or even fanciful, it allowed my friend to engage his faith while in a tough marketplace environment. My friend was able to create a safe, spiritual, embryonic place for him to commune with God amid the seedy culture in which he found himself.

Some might argue that my friend's thoughts would diminish a broker's effectiveness. Investing is, after all, a cutthroat business. Only the aggressive and doggedly determined succeed. However, as I mentioned, my friend has remained a successful broker. In fact, one could argue that he is even more successful than he was before. His client base has remained strong, and his clients trust him. He has produced well for them, despite the economic ups and downs of the past few decades. By our culture's standard, he is successful. More importantly, he is successful by God's standard: "If there is any excellence . . ."

In the New Testament book of Colossians, God calls us to a high level of excellence in our vocational lives. He says, "Whatever you do, work heartily, as for the Lord and not for men, knowing that from the Lord you will receive the inheritance as your reward. You are serving the Lord Christ" (3:23–24). My friend has experienced this. We can too.

Excellence Everywhere

When Philippians calls us to excellence using the conditional "if," it doesn't mean that Christians rarely achieve excellence. It means that excellence must be attained using the biblically guided and Spirit-empowered tools that God provides. This applies to every area of our lives. The late Martin Luther King Jr. expressed this concept of excellence so well while speaking to a group of young people in a public school six months before his assassination:

> If it falls your lot to be a street sweeper, sweep streets like
> Michelangelo painted pictures, sweep streets like Beethoven

composed music, sweep streets like Leontyne Price sings before the Metropolitan Opera. Sweep streets like Shakespeare wrote poetry. Sweep streets so well that all the hosts of heaven and earth will have to pause and say: Here lived a great street sweeper who swept his job well.⁹

The Bible has a lot to say on almost every issue we deal with in our fallen world. We have no excuse for failing to be biblically guided in our excellence. Through the Bible, God encourages parents to provide love to their children, not to provoke them to outbursts of anger, and to give rightly placed discipline and direction (see Prov. 22:6; Eph. 6:4). God calls husbands and wives to mutual submission, strong communication, selfless love, and security-producing faithfulness (see Prov. 5:15–23; Eph. 5:21–33). God guides us to approach our personal finances by avoiding unnecessary debt, enjoying our blessings, providing for our families, and having a generous, giving spirit (see Ps. 37:21; Eccles. 5:19; Rom. 13:8; 1 Tim. 5:8). Through the Bible, God directs us to be free from vulgarity, to encourage others, and to speak truth to one another (see Eph. 4:15, 29; James 3:2–12). God teaches us to use our physical bodies well, to take care of them but not to put too much premium on them to the point of body worship and the subjugation of our souls (see 1 Cor. 6:19; 1 Tim. 4:8).

What is important to note in each of these examples is the precise direction the Bible provides. The Bible provides laser-beam focus in the form of truth and guidance. We are not left to wonder what excellence looks like in each of these areas. The list goes on: business ethics, bioethics, retirement, conflict resolution, dealing with damaged emotions, sexuality, educational priorities, the use of the arts—and a host of other areas.

Contrary to what some might think, the Bible gives sound teaching and clear guidance in so many areas of life. Similarly, the Holy Spirit lives within you empowering you to live according to the Bible's guidance (1 Cor. 3:16; John 16:13). Excellence is truly within our grasp. There are quite a few whatevers to consider as we think about excellence throughout our day. Excellence begins with learning to think the way God wants us to think. "If there is any excellence . . . think about these things."

9

YOUR ACE IN THE HOLE

The Twin Tunnels of Praise

"If there is anything worthy of praise . . ."

You take approximately 23,000 breaths every day, but when was the last time you thanked God for one of them?

Mark Batterson

Of all the words we have looked at in Philippians 4:8, none is more positive and uplifting than our final word, *praise*. We love this word. We lavish praise on our kids. Bosses praise their employees when they do a good job. Pet owners praise their pets when they listen to them. Crowds praise superstar athletes when they excel. Even Hollywood elites praise each other at award banquets. Everyone likes to be praised for something, and we don't mind praising others when they deserve to be praised. It should not surprise us, then, that

151

thinking about things that are worthy of praise concludes God's top eight list of ways to think.

The lavishing of praise can either make or break a person's spirit in this life. Most of us remember times we either received praise for something we did or did not receive praise when we desperately needed it.

I vividly remember experiences of both receiving praise and not receiving it early in my ministry. When I graduated from seminary almost thirty years ago, I landed a one-year internship at a large, prominent church in the Midwest. Back then there were not too many megachurches. This one was huge, and the internship was a unique opportunity for a young man wet behind the ears. On the first day, the other interns and I were addressed via recorded video by the businessman who was single-handedly funding our year at this megachurch. After singing the praises of the church, he challenged us to give it our all and to make the most of our time there. He shared with us that when the year was up, he didn't want our boss to write a recommendation for us saying that we "tried our best" but that we were "performers." He closed his video message by looking directly at the camera and saying, "Don't screw up." As I drove home that evening, I didn't know if I was at a church internship program, a General Electric corporate training program, or boot camp for the military. One thing I did know: I was now in the deep end of the pool, and I needed to swim for all I was worth.

That year proved to be one of the most daunting and difficult years of my life. As a young man with a heart that was tender for God and for people and who at the same time was susceptible to a bit of performance anxiety, I had a hard time embracing the motto this church chose for my class of interns: "Perform with Excellence." I wasn't an actor on a stage. I was a burgeoning pastor and teacher. I didn't go to seminary to be the next pastoral version of Jack Welch (or Elon Musk, if you are a millennial) but to be a shepherd of the flock of God. Don't get me wrong. I believe in excellence and realize most pastors need to learn a thing or two. Our calling, however, is not about excellence first but about love first. It's not about performing as much as pastoring. Looking back, I'm not sure this church had its priorities in the right order at that time.

I struggled that year. I felt overwhelmed in that fast-paced, high-octane, take-no-spiritual-prisoners type of church. It didn't fit my temperament very well, at least not in that season of my life. I'm sure those around me sensed my feelings. I had more questions than answers about the nature of church. I felt deeply called, but I lacked confidence. I also had some internal issues, born of unresolved childhood pain, which created insecurity in my soul. As one wanting to be a faithful shepherd, I needed some shepherding myself.

Toward the end of that year, as things were winding down, two of my superiors personally shared their perspective of my ministry performance with me. One was deflating. The other was inflating. One had the power to take the wind out of my sails. The other had the power to propel me into open waters. One lacked praise. The other was filled with praise. I will never forget either.

As I sat in the office of the first supervisor, he shared with me an illustration I believe he thought was truthful and helpful. He said that my year at his church was like playing in the major leagues. I was with him so far. No argument. Then he said that my batting average was pretty low. He threw out a number, and it was below .200. Not good for a professional baseball player or a pastor. He then tried to encourage me. He said, "Wherever you end up next year will be like the minor leagues, and I'm confident you will bat much better." I would later learn that this is what is called a "backhanded compliment." It's like saying, "For a fat person, you don't sweat much." His message was clear: I had struck out in the majors and now was destined for the minors. I think he meant well. He was trying to set me up for a future of success. But his message made me feel deflated. As I walked out of his office, I felt that maybe church work was not for me. That night was long, and the week was even longer.

However, God is good, and praise is a powerful restorer. About a week later, one of my other supervisors asked me to teach a lesson in his ministry. I would be doing so in front of about three hundred people. I had never taught a group that size. I prepared hard. I prayed hard. Then I delivered my lesson. As the crowd cleared out, my supervisor came up to me and said, "I sat in the back and listened to your talk. I was a little nervous for you. I was unsure how it was going to go. But within three minutes of the start of your talk, I knew you had the goods. I sat back, breathed a sigh of relief, and enjoyed what you had to say. Great job! You're going to make a great pastor." After a week of wondering if I should jump ship, the wind was back in my sails. Praise had done its job. It tends to work that way.

The fact that I remember both of those encounters almost thirty years later reveals the power of praise. Maybe you have similar memories of your own personal encounters. Praise is a powerful motivator. Its opposite has the power to demotivate. Thinking about "anything worthy of praise" is important because much is at stake concerning praise's use or lack thereof.

"If There Is Anything Worthy of Praise"

The word before us is the Greek word *epainos* (pronounced *EH-pie-nahs*), consistently translated as "praise." It was a relatively common word and carried with it the dual ideas of "recognition"[1] and "approval"[2]: recognizing what was good and true followed by showing approval. When that happened, praise ensued. Like shining a spotlight on the center act on a stage, praise shines a light so that all may see what is worth seeing. It says, "Look at that! Isn't that awesome? Wow!" That's praise.

Given this understanding, we can praise just about anything. We can recognize and approve of so many things in the world around us. From a nice car to a majestic mountain to a beloved pet to a well-run business, everything is open to praise. We can choose to be "praise machines" if we want to—praising just about anything and everything we see. Some of us might even know people who are like this. They are constantly praising the people and the things around them, and their praise knows no boundaries. Though they are certainly people who tend to see things in a positive light, throwing praise around too liberally can water down this powerful trait. The Bible, in all its rich wisdom, reserves praise for only two groups: God and people.

Epainos is used ten times in the New Testament. On five occasions, the New Testament writers broke into praise of God. They recognized and approved of his goodness and glory (see Eph. 1:6, 12, 14; Phil. 1:11; 1 Pet. 1:7). On the other occasions, people were the object of praise. Three times people praised the behavior of other people (see Rom. 13:3; 2 Cor. 8:18; 1 Pet. 2:14), and two times God praised people for their actions (see Rom. 2:29; 1 Cor. 4:5). God and people are the two objects worthy of our recognition and approval. So when Philippians 4:8 challenges us to think about "anything worthy of praise," we are asked to travel through the twin tunnels of divine and human praise.

The Pathway to Praise

We are to think about praise. We are to view the world around us through the lens of divine and human praise. What does this entail? How is this accomplished? A clear and well-traversed pathway guides our thinking that leads to praise. It looks like this:

Appraise ⟶ Approve ⟶ Applause

Building one upon another, the three aspects of this biblical pathway allow us to work our way toward praise in our thoughts and perspectives. This pathway provides a profound journey toward praise if we are willing to travel it. Let's take the journey.

Appraise

We begin by appraising what is going on around us. We analyze what we see, hear, and experience. We size up our environment. To accomplish this, we need to apply what the Bible calls "discernment." Proverbs 14:8 warns, "The wisdom of the prudent is to discern his way, but the folly of fools is deceiving." Part of wisdom is the ability to discern—to distinguish between good and bad, truth and falsehood. Discernment involves asking the right questions and making the right judgments. If we fail to do this, we can become deceived and get off track.

Mary, Jesus's mother, had to use discernment when the angel Gabriel appeared to her to announce the birth of Jesus. Gabriel introduced his arrival with these words to Mary: "Greetings, O favored one, the Lord is with you!" (Luke 1:28). Understandably, she was a bit unnerved. Who wouldn't be? She didn't know what to make of these words. What was the angel getting at? The Bible reports that she quickly moved into discernment mode: "She was greatly troubled at the saying, and tried to discern what sort of greeting this might be" (Luke 1:29). Her mental wheels were turning. She was sizing up the angel's greeting and sorting through all the options. *Why am I favored? How is the Lord with me? Am I in trouble? Does God want something?* She was appraising. She was discerning. Eventually, the angel clarified his message for Mary. He let her know that she would be the one to bring the long-awaited Savior into the world. Mary's discernment, however, was a critical part of the equation. It helped her appraise the angel's words. And it would soon lead Mary to full-throttle praise (see Luke 1:46–55).

We use various tools to discern and appraise. We use the Bible as a guide to know what is good and right. We use our rational minds to assess what makes sense. We use the help of others, what the Bible calls "counsel," to bolster our discernment (see Prov. 15:22). We want to be careful that our appraisal is solid and substantive. Most importantly, the Spirit works through God's Word, our rational minds, and others to help us rightly size up the things we encounter. He helps us to know who and when to praise. As the Bible explains, "The natural person does not accept the things of the Spirit of God, for they are folly to him, and he is not able to understand them because they are spiritually discerned. The spiritual person judges all things" (1 Cor. 2:14–15). We can have confidence that, as we follow the Lord, he will give us discernment as we appraise.

I constantly appraise the world around me. Doing so is a part of learning to think as God wants me to think. I am constantly assessing, discerning, and appraising

- as my kids share things with me,
- as my wife lives out her life in front of me,
- as my friends interact with me,
- as my church members interface with one another and the culture around them,
- as my neighbors come and go,
- as God moves in and through my life.

As a result, I have the opportunity to distinguish between what is good and right and what is not so good and right. I am able to discern truth and error—what is beneficial to my soul and what is harmful. Doing so allows me to move on to the second leg of the journey toward praise.

Approve

Once we have discerned what is good and right around us, we are ready to take an important emotional step of approving what we have appraised. This is a critical part of the pathway to praise. It allows us to transfer what our minds have discerned to be worthy of praise to our hearts. It allows us to take what began as a cerebral exercise into the "cardiac aspect" of our personhood. It allows us to begin to *feel* something about what we are going to praise.

Approval is a powerful force. During my internship, I *felt* disapproval from one supervisor and approval from another. The difference was stark. One was a downer, and the other was an upper. Both disapproval and approval dramatically affected me on a *feeling* level. Approval works this way because we are hardwired as humans created in God's image as relational beings. Approval is the validation and affirmation of relationship, and we experience these relational connections in deeply personal, emotional ways. Once we latch on to this reality of approval and its power on a visceral level, we can see praise beginning to form.

An instructive story tucked away in the Old Testament reveals the power of approval. While on the run from King Saul, the soon-to-be-king David experienced the tension between approval and disapproval. At one point, David aligned himself with an ally named Achish, who partnered with the Philistines against Saul, and together they were about to go into battle. However, the Philistines rightly discerned that David's popularity was growing and that he could eventually turn on them in favor of Israel. This made the Philistines leery. Achish wanted David in the battle against Saul. The Philistines didn't. What happened next reveals what's at stake with approval and disapproval:

> Then Achish called David and said to him, "As the LORD lives, you have been honest, and to me it seems right that you

should march out and in with me in the campaign. For I have found nothing wrong in you from the day of your coming to me to this day. Nevertheless, the lords do not approve of you." (1 Sam. 29:6)

The Philistines appraised David and disapproved of his involvement, fearing that he might become stronger and turn on them. Achish appraised David and found him honest to the point that it seemed right to bring him along. The reality is that both appraisals were correct! David would be a great asset to Achish in the battle, but he also would eventually become stronger and turn on the Philistines (remember that David had brutally defeated the Philistine giant Goliath). Both appraisals were spot-on. One led to approval and the other to disapproval. David felt the support of Achish and resented the disapproval of the Philistines.

Approval tends to work this way. Approval is an emotionally charged interaction that bridges appraisal with praise. Disapproval is an equally emotionally charged interaction that burns the bridge between appraisal and praise. The point is that without approval there is not going to be praise, but with approval praise is right around the corner.

In thinking about what is worthy to be praised, we need to approve what we appraise. Doing so adds the necessary emotional edge that makes praise so powerful. When my supervisor came up to me that day and shared words of affirmation based on my talk, I could feel the weight of his approval. His praise was laden with it. Similarly, when we praise God for his goodness and actions, he can tell whether our praise is bathed in emotional approval or whether we are simply going through the motions. This is why some

Christians raise their arms in worship. Their genuine praise is riding on the emotional wave of their approval of the goodness and greatness of God.

Without the step of approval, our praise will be paltry, shallow, and maybe even nonexistent. With it, we are ready for the third and final step that brings praise to fullness.

Applause

If appraisal is a mental activity and approval is an emotional activity, then applause, the third and final leg of our journey toward praise, is clearly the action step. This is where praise comes to fruition as we display it in tangible ways. This is where praise is presented through an act of our will. This is where applause springs forth from approval and becomes praise.

Many of the Psalms of the Old Testament were written by King David, and they are some of the most intimate and personal writings of the Bible. They are by and large poems, letters, and songs written to and about God. We should not be surprised, then, that they are filled with praise. In fact, the word *praise* appears just shy of 140 times in the Psalms. What is most fascinating, however, is the various forms praise can take:

For this I will praise you, O LORD, . . . and sing to your name. (18:49)

Shout for joy in the LORD. . . . Praise befits the upright. (33:1)

My tongue shall tell of your righteousness and of your praise all the day long. (35:28)

Clap your hands. . . . Sing praises to God. (47:1, 6)

Silence is praise to you, Zion-dwelling God. (65:1 Message)

Accept my freewill offerings of praise, O LORD. (119:108)

Lift up your hands in the sanctuary and praise the LORD. (134:2 NIV)

Let them praise his name with dancing. (149:3)

Praise him with trumpet . . . lute . . . harp . . . tambourine . . . strings . . . loud clashing cymbals! (150:3–5)

Singing, shouting, telling, clapping, giving, lifting hands, dancing, playing instruments—and even, at times, silence— are all appropriate responses to our appraisal and approval of God, responses that reveal the fullness of praise. Through these responses we know that we have finally arrived at praise.

In All Things, Give Praise

As mentioned earlier, the New Testament is clear that the praise we are to think about should follow the twin tunnels of God and people. God is after relationality in our think-ing. Throughout each day, we are to have a mindset that leads us to erupt in praise as we interact with God and the people around us. We are to appraise, approve, and applaud whenever we find something associated with God and others that is worthy of praise. When we see praise in this light, we realize we have dozens, if not hundreds, of opportunities to truly "think praise" throughout the day.

Think about all the things you encounter that provide you with a chance to break out in praise: a majestic nature scene in God's creation, the birth of a baby, a promotion at work that happens because of the sovereign blessing of God, an answered prayer, a restored marriage, a child or grandchild who finally sees the light and gets on the right path, peace that surpasses understanding in the midst of chaos, a kind word from a coworker or a friend, a song you like in church, an insight you get from reading the Bible, even the eternal homegoing of a loved one. These are all examples of the opportunities you and I have to "think praise." There are so many in a single day. Some are big. Some are small. Each one provides an opportunity to appraise, approve, and applaud.

Whether it be to God or to other people, we have plenty of reasons to give thanks and praise. This is why the apostle Paul exhorted us, "Give thanks in all circumstances; for this is the will of God in Christ Jesus for you" (1 Thess. 5:18). Even as the psalmist contemplated his own existence during a quiet moment, he erupted in praise when he wrote, "I praise you, for I am fearfully and wonderfully made. Wonderful are your works; my soul knows it very well" (139:14). Thoughts like these are bound to enhance our thinking too. They keep us from settling for anything less in life than to think richly and fully about God and those around us. As the author G. K. Chesterton said so well, "The worst moment for the atheist is when he is really thankful and and has nobody to thank."[3] When God is in the picture, we always have someone to praise.

Our Ace in the Hole

Here is one final thought about praise. It's something I have learned from being a follower of Jesus for more than thirty-five years. When all else fails—when the other seven lines of thinking seem to fall short—praise will always do the trick. What I mean by this is that there are times when we are fighting the good fight of faith in our daily walk and not a lot seems to be falling into place. We are trying to think about whatever is true, looking for the intersection of God's transcendent truth and our personal truth, but we can't seem to find it. We are trying to think honorably and be nonreactionary, but knee-jerk thinking seems to be winning the day. We are trying to be biblically guided and Spirit empowered in our pursuit of excellence in our thinking, but the flesh is putting up quite a fight. We are trying to avoid settling in our thinking, following the dictates laid out in Philippians 4:8, but for whatever reason, our thoughts aren't cooperating. We are having a bad day.

Here is what I have learned. Even when nothing else is working, we can praise. We can *choose* to praise. We can appraise, approve, and applaud. This is a choice we have each moment of each day. The ability to choose to praise is within our power, our Spirit-enabled will, no matter what.

I have a dear friend whom I have known for almost two decades. She had both a difficult childhood and a difficult early adulthood that were traumatic in the worst sense. When she was twelve years old, her family was on a vacation at the beach, and she wandered off alone for a walk. She met two older men who invited her back to their tent. Naïve and trusting, she went. The next hour was the worst of her life. After being sexually abused and having her innocence violently taken away, she ran back to her family's campsite and told her parents what had happened. They took her to a nearby hospital, had her treated, and filed a police report. The men were never caught. Thinking they were doing the right thing, her parents decided to put the nightmare behind them and never talk about it again. This tactic may have worked for them, but it didn't work for her.

As my friend matured into a young woman, she developed serious emotional and relationship problems. She found solace in food and became obese. She couldn't find intimacy with a man in a healthy relationship. She found a career as a schoolteacher, and everyone loved her. She was a great teacher and had an incredible love for children. Nobody understood why she carried so much weight and never married. But she knew. The nightmare had never left her.

Eventually, the dam holding back all the physical, emotional, and psychological trauma broke. The pain became too intense, and she decided to address what she called the elephant in the room. Through years of counseling and the love of family and close friends, bathed in the grace of God, she found a pronounced level of healing. She addressed the underlying issue of childhood sexual abuse, got control of her eating addiction, and eventually found a safe and tender man whom she married. Hers is an amazing story of tragedy turned into triumph.

Even so, she still has difficult days. In a fallen world filled with fallen bodies and minds, few of us ever experience a complete and full recovery from such things. One day in church, as I was sitting in the front row, I noticed her a few rows over standing with her husband as we were singing.

She stood with arms lifted high in praise to God and tears running down her face. The tears didn't look like tears of happiness but of sadness.

After the service, I went up to her and asked her how she was doing. She said she was okay. I asked her if it was a tough day. She knew what I meant. She said, "Yes, it's a tough day." What she said next blew me away and allowed me to make sense of her tears. She said, "The pain is here today, but I choose joy." I *choose* joy. In the midst of pain. Her tears were clearly a mixture of pain and joy, all jumbled together. She was in a battle. Old feelings were welling, but with the power of praise fueling her spirit, there was also joy. And her tears expressed both. She chose joy. I have never forgotten this.

You and I might never have to face the kind of abuse my friend had to endure. At least I hope not. But we have our own issues. They are real to us. They too can create some difficult days, the kind of days in which we struggle to apply the kind of thinking that can produce peace in our souls. Our ace in the hole is praise.

"The pain is here today, but I choose joy."

10

A PEACE-DRIVEN LIFE

Getting the Most Out of Your Thinking

> "Think about these things . . .
> and the God of peace will be with you."

The most holy practice, the nearest to daily life, and the most essential for the spiritual life, is the practice of the presence of God.

Brother Lawrence

My wife and I have three adult children. We love each of them equally but differently. Part of the reason for this is how different they are from each other. Our two oldest are girls. They are separated by about two years. When they were three and one, my wife nicknamed them "Pastel" and "Technicolor." The older was soft, gentle, and delicate, while the younger was bright, crisp, and colorful. They haven't

167

changed in twenty-five years. When "Technicolor" was thirteen or fourteen, her grandpa promised to take her for a canoe ride on his lake. For various reasons, it didn't happen. That same year I promised to take her rock climbing. Again, for various reasons, it didn't happen. She has never let us forget it. Even to this day she comments on the broken promises of that summer. They have become a source of family humor. Someday I need to take her rock climbing.

Promises are tricky. We love the idea of them, but we are simultaneously leery of them, for good reason. Most of us have been promised something by someone only to have them not come through. We let each other down, sometimes in small ways, such as failing to take someone canoeing or rock climbing, but sometimes in much bigger ways, such as failing to uphold our marital vows. Most of us long for lives of promises kept but are skeptical that people are able to keep them. Life can be difficult in a fallen world filled with less-than-perfect people.

One thing I love about God is that he always keeps his promises. As the Bible expresses so wonderfully, "For all the promises of God find their Yes in [Jesus]. That is why it is through him that we utter our Amen to God for his glory" (2 Cor. 1:20). God is always true to his word. God never fails to deliver what he says he will deliver. He always comes through on his end.

The Promise for Those Who Want Joy

Though the bulk of this book has been centered on one verse from the Bible, to fully understand the fullness of this verse, we must complete our journey by briefly looking at the next one, for that verse contains the promise for those who learn to think the way God prescribes. God makes a promise to those who spend their lives focused on the eight lines of thought laid out in Philippians 4:8. The promise of Philippians 4:9 is this: "What you have learned and received and heard and seen in me—practice these things, and the God of peace will be with you."

At first glance, some might think this verse is not connected with verse 8. They might be tempted to think this verse introduces a new topic. This is not the case. After explaining the eight lines of thought in verse 8, Paul the apostle now challenges us to be like him. He is essentially saying that he is committed to living his life with these eight perspectives in mind, and he challenges us to pattern our lives after his. What we have learned and received from his writings, what we have heard and seen in the things he has said and done, we are to "practice these things." These "things" are clearly tied to verse 8. They refer to the eight ways of thinking he outlined in the previous verse.

At this point, he moves on to the resulting promise associated with learning to think as God wants us to think: "and the God of peace will be with you." There is a specificity associated with this promise we don't want to miss. To better reveal the precise promise that you could otherwise overlook, the verse might be most grammatically straightforward translated this way: "And the God, who is peace, will be with you." Notice that the core of the promise is not peace but God, who brings peace. The promise is the very presence of God, a God who "will be with you" as a result of your learning to embrace his prescribed way of thinking.

The Promise Is Presence

The promise of God's presence is a profound promise. In the Christian life, we might be tempted to seek after all the potential blessings God may or may not provide. Financial security, a good job, children who never wander from the faith, a fulfilling marriage, emotions that never turn to depression or anxiety, trouble-free neighbors, or a hassle-free church are all examples of the "good life" many Christians shoot for in their journey of following the Lord. We pray for these things. We work hard for them. We even trust God to provide them based on our faithfulness and obedience. At the end of the day, however, none of these things are guaranteed by God in this fallen world. He does not promise us any of them for a life well lived. But he does promise us his presence.

God's presence—the reality that he is "with us"—is the most meaningful and powerful gift God could give us in response to our right thinking. It is more important than any of the above-mentioned blessings we tend to seek. In fact, these other blessings pale in comparison to the actual presence of God with us. Our souls are hardwired to desire God's presence more than anything else. Some of us just have never seen it this way or dug deep enough in our souls to realize it.

Think of the person you love to be with the most. Think of the person whose presence consistently lifts your spirit. Fix in your mind the person you most look forward to being with, the person whose presence you both enjoy and long for. That person might be your spouse or your child. Maybe that person is a hunting buddy, a workout partner, or a childhood friend. Now imagine that you entered a sweepstakes and won

170

an all-expenses-paid trip to an exotic destination like Tahiti (assuming you like tropical climates). As is true of most trips won in a sweepstakes, you can bring a friend with you. You immediately think of your favorite person. You can't wait to go with them. It's going to be a great time.

Now imagine that as you are reading the fine print on your sweepstakes entry form, you notice a special clause that reads, "If you choose not to bring another person, you can receive upgraded travel arrangements and upgraded accommodations at the destination site." Who doesn't like an upgrade on an airplane, especially on a transpacific flight? Who doesn't like an upgraded hotel room? For a split second, you give thought to these upgrades in lieu of bringing your friend. But only for a split second. The vast majority of us would opt for a friend's companionship over the upgrades. Why? Because presence is more desirable than tangible blessings.

It's important we see God and his presence this way, especially in light of the tangible blessings we all desire. From God's vantage point, the tangible blessings of life are similar to the upgrades in the sweepstakes scenario. I know it's hard for many blessings-laden Americans to understand this, but when God views our lives from the perspective of eternity and with the desire for us to want to know and trust him more than anything else, he sees our chasing after the good life as similar to the chasing after upgrades on a trip to Tahiti. What matters more than anything else is the trip and who is with us, not the upgrades. What matters to God more than anything else is our journey toward knowing and experiencing him, not the blessings that may or may not come with it. What saddens God the most is that many well-meaning Christians would be tempted to trade his presence in exchange for blessings.

171

Please don't get me wrong here. There is nothing wrong with blessings, especially blessings that have to do with a fulfilling marriage, successful parenting, joy-filled emotions, a nice retirement, and a good church to call our spiritual home. These are all wonderful things. But they are ultimately unfulfilling without God's presence. Of course it's great when we have blessings *and* presence. However, the point of verse 9 and much of the teaching of the Bible is that the presence is promised, but the tangible blessings are not. Blessings are not even mentioned in Philippians 4:9. We will experience times in our lives when the blessings don't flow as we think they should. The promise, however, still stands. Those who learn to think as God has directed—about whatever is true, honorable, just, pure, lovely, commendable, excellent, and worthy of praise—will be graced with an experiential sense that the God of peace is with them. This is more powerful than anything a blessings-laden life can provide. Presence always trumps blessings. God's promise is his presence.

The Purpose of Presence

When I was a burgeoning teenager on the cusp of adolescence, I went through a time of pronounced anxiety. I was in junior high, and like many kids at that age, I was deeply insecure about my changing body, whether I was liked at school, and what the future held for me. Mind you, I couldn't consciously process or verbalize any of these feelings, and this is why they presented themselves as a generalized anxiety at that time in my life. Many kids go through a similar experience, and they each respond differently.

I can remember a period of time in seventh grade when I did not want to go to school. I would wake up with a foreboding sense of dread about the day ahead. Claiming a stomachache, I would tell my parents I was sick and had to stay home. The only problem was that my dad was old school. He had been born in the middle of the Great Depression and had pulled himself up by his bootstraps, so to speak. His twofold criteria for being sick was a high fever and vomiting, two things that are hard to fake. Stomachaches never satisfied his criteria. I was out the door and off to school, with anxiety and dread leading the way.

As I look back on how I got through that time, I see that two things made all the difference on a daily level. The first was music. You may have heard the saying "Music hath charms to soothe a savage breast." Music can take the primitive, rough parts of the soul and smooth them out. This proved true for me. Playing the piano and listening to music took the edge off my anxiety during my difficult days as a young teenager. This is why I so appreciate music still today.

The other thing that got me through this time was the anticipated presence of my mom at the end of each school day. Dad was the one who forced me to go to school. He was always the disciplinarian, and for that I am grateful. Every kid needs discipline or they will end up being an irresponsible and immature adult. Mom, however, was empathetic to my emotions and understood what I was experiencing (even more than I did at that age). At the beginning of each day, as I would tepidly leave the house, she would say to me, "I will be here when you get home. Don't worry. I will be waiting." Throughout the day, when I would feel anxiety and fear rising up in my soul, I would think about my mom waiting for me. I would picture her at our kitchen table with a glass of milk and a cookie in front of her. Just the thought of her presence would stem the tide of my anxiety. The eventual experience of her presence would bring profound relief. We would talk about my day. We would share a snack. After all these years, I don't remember the gist of our conversations, but I do remember the feeling of her presence and the relief it created in my soul.

Presence is powerful. It breeds security, it heals wounds, and it fosters perseverance. In short, presence brings peace. This has been my experience from an early age. The presence of a trusted person truly is one of the most crucial things our souls need. Maybe now we can all understand why it leaves the "lesser blessings" in the dust. Maybe now we can understand why the promise of verse 9 is so radical and life altering: "And the God of peace will be with you." This special sense of God's presence is reserved for those who draw close to him as they learn to think in new and fresh ways. Now that is worth pursuing.

The Missing Link

Most people don't realize the link between perspective and peace. They don't understand that the right kind of thinking about the world around us—about our lives, others, and even God—produces a steadiness of spirit. Philippians 4:8–9 tells us that as we learn to craft the kind of daily mindset that follows the pathways laid out by God, these pathways will lead to peace—peace found in the special presence of God with us.

This presence and peace come to us in two distinct ways as we learn to think as God wants us to think.

1. They come to us as a natural result of aligning our thinking with the good things of God. This only makes sense. As we focus on things that are true, honorable, just, pure, lovely, commendable, excellent, and worthy of praise, it is bound to have a positive, peaceful effect on our souls. Naturally.

2. They come to us as a special impartation directly from God. In other words, God imparts a special grace to us when we learn to think as he wants us to think. God gives us the grace of his presence and peace.

Either way, naturally or through special impartation, we receive the missing link that so many are searching for. Peace through presence, found as a result of following God in our thinking.

My hope is that as we spend the remainder of our days on earth learning to follow God's way of thinking, we will find deeper levels of peace through God's abiding presence. No missed canoe rides here. No forgotten rock climbing excursions with God. He is always true to his Word. Let's learn to think differently.

AFTERWORD

A businessman once told his staff that if they couldn't put an idea or a proposal on a single page, it wasn't worth presenting. This is a tough challenge after writing a full-length book. Even so, the principle still holds true. Let's distill what we have discovered so that we will be able to remember the main ideas behind each mindset.

- *The power of a biblical "whatever"*: It is impossible to exaggerate the extent to which good, godly thoughts can influence your perspective and outlook. Imagine the possibilities if you begin to think as God thinks. Imagine all the "whatevers." Life is filled with them.

- *Whatever is true*: Find God at the intersection of transcendent truth and personal truth. Allow God's unchanging reality, as it intersects with your reality, to bring definition, clarity, and meaning to your personal experiences and perceptions.

- *Whatever is honorable*: Learn to develop a nonreactionary spirit. Count to five . . . or five thousand if necessary. Give God's Spirit time to gain control over your first-impulse reactions, to give you his wisdom, and to sustain you.

- *Whatever is just*: Do right through righting wrongs; make right through forgiving wrongs. Be on the lookout for the injustices that grieve you, because they grieve God. While you're at it, be kind. Learn to forgive. Don't be an either/or agent of justice; rather, be a both/and Christ follower.

- *Whatever is pure*: Prioritize relational purity by following Christ's example of love. Healthy relationships with others are most available as the overflow from having a healthy relationship with God.

- *Whatever is lovely*: Seek legitimate pleasure in the right places. Nurture safe-harbor relationships and solid activities. Keep a sound view of God, and always give more than you get.

- *Whatever is commendable*: Create a good reputation that links your behavior with others' assessments. Because you can control only the half of this equation that focuses on your behavior, commit to faithfulness, kindness, righteousness, and honor.

- *If there is any excellence*: Become biblically guided and Spirit empowered in all you do. You find and experience excellence when you live by faith in the power of the Spirit, guided by God's Word.

- *If there is anything worthy of praise*: Seek to appraise, approve, and applaud God and others. Praise God through all the opportunities he gives you.

Dream about and envision all the possibilities associated with thinking along these eight lines. And they carry a promise: the experienced presence of God and his peace.

NOTES

Introduction

1. Jason G. Goldman, "Why Bronze Medalists Are Happier than Silver Winners," *Scientific American*, August 9, 2012, http://blogs.scientific american.com/thoughtful-animal/2012/08/09/why-bronze-medalists-are -happier-than-silver-winners.

Chapter 1 The Power of a Biblical "Whatever"

1. Johannes P. Louw and Eugene A. Nida, eds., *Greek-English Lexicon of the New Testament: Based on Semantic Domains* (New York: United Bible Societies, 1989), s.v. "hosos."

2. "Prevalence of Self-Reported Aggressive Driving Behavior: United States, 2014," AAA Foundation for Traffic Safety, July 10, 2016, https:// aaafoundation.org/prevalence-self-reported-aggressive-driving-behavior -united-states-2014/.

Chapter 2 Two Ways of Seeing

1. Gerhard Kittel, Gerhard Friedrich, and Geoffrey W. Bromiley, eds., *Theological Dictionary of the New Testament* (Grand Rapids: Eerdmans, 1984), s.v. "alethes."

2. Kittel, Friedrich, and Bromiley, eds., *Theological Dictionary of the New Testament*, s.v. "alethes."

3. C. S. Lewis, *Surprised by Joy: The Shape of My Early Life* (Boston: Houghton Mifflin Harcourt, 1966).

Chapter 3 Calm, Cool, Collected

1. Kittel, Friedrich, and Bromiley, eds., *Theological Dictionary of the New Testament*, s.v. "semnos."

2. John Piper, "A Call for Coronary Christians," Desiring God, January 23, 2002, http://www.desiringgod.org/articles/a-call-for-coronary-christians.

3. Piper, "A Call for Coronary Christians."

4. Piper, "A Call for Coronary Christians."

5. Thomas Jefferson, quoted in Jon Meacham, *Thomas Jefferson: The Art of Power* (New York: Random House, 2012), 237.

6. Thomas Jefferson, quoted in Meacham, *Thomas Jefferson*, 236.

Chapter 4 Thoughts That Heal

1. Douglas Mangum, Rachel Klippenstein, Derek R. Brown, and Rebekah Hurst, eds., *Lexham Theological Wordbook* (Bellingham, WA: Lexingham Press, 2014), s.v. "dikaios."

2. Kittel, Friedrich, and Bromiley, eds., *Theological Dictionary of the New Testament*, s.v., "dikaios."

3. Titled *Nicomachean Ethics*.

4. Jennifer Riley, "Nothing More Radical than Bible in Injustice Fight, Says Tutu," *Christian Post*, September 8, 2008, http://www.christianpost.com/news/nothing-more-radical-than-bible-in-injustice-fight-says-tutu-34177/.

5. "Famous Twain Quotes," The Mark Twain House & Museum, February 2, 2018, http://www.twainquotes.com/Right.html.

6. See www.thebekindpeopleproject.org.

7. Nicholas Kristof, "Evangelicals without Blowhards," *New York Times*, July 30, 2011, http://www.nytimes.com/2011/07/31/opinion/sunday/kristof-evangelicals-without-blowhards.html.

Chapter 5 The Myth of Individual Holiness

1. R. L. Thomas, *New American Standard Hebrew-Aramaic and Greek Dictionaries: Updated Edition* (La Habra, CA: Foundation Publications, 1998), s.v. "hagnos."

2. C. S. Lewis, *Mere Christianity* (New York: Macmillan, 1978), 153.

3. Larry Crabb, *A Different Kind of Happiness: Discovering the Joy that Comes from Sacrificial Love* (Grand Rapids: Baker Books, 2016), 46.

4. Robert G. Clouse, "Recent Premillennialism: Late Great Predictions," *Christian History* 61 (1999), https://www.christianhistoryinstitute.org/magazine/article/recent-premillennialism-late-great-predictions/.

5. Robert D. Putnam and David E. Campbell, *American Grace: How Religion Divides and Unites Us* (New York: Simon & Schuster, 2010), 81.

6. "Database of Megachurches in the U.S.," Hartford Institute for Religion Research, November 22, 2011, http://hirr.hartsem.edu/megachurch/database.html.

7. Thom S. Rainer, "Seven Updated Trends on Megachurches in America," *Christian Post*, September 19, 2012, http://www.christianpost.com/news/seven-updated-trends-on-megachurches-in-america-81860/.

8. "Fast Facts about American Religion," Hartford Institute for Religion Research, September 3, 2005, http://hirr.hartsem.edu/research/fastfacts/fast_facts.html.

9. Alan Hirsch, "Defining Missional," *Christianity Today Online*, Fall 2008, http://www.christianitytoday.com/pastors/2008/fall/17.20.html.

Chapter 6 Christian Hedonists

1. *Merriam-Webster's Collegiate Dictionary*, 11th ed. (2003), s.v. "pleasure."

2. Kittel, Friedrich, and Bromiley, eds., *Theological Dictionary of the New Testament*, s.v. "phileo."

3. R. Jamieson, A. R. Fausset, and D. Brown, *Commentary Critical and Explanatory on the Whole Bible* (Grand Rapids: Eerdmans, 1935), Logos Research Systems ebook, s.v. "phileo."

4. Glenn Frey and Jackson Browne, "Take It Easy," on *Eagles*, performed by the Eagles, recorded 1972, Olympic Studios, London.

5. John Piper, *Desiring God: Meditations of a Christian Hedonist* (New York: Crown Publishing Group, 2010), 18.

Chapter 7 Your Life on a Billboard

1. Wikipedia, s.v. "John Grisham," last modified June 7, 2017, https://en.wikipedia.org/wiki/John_Grisham.

2. Sammy McDavid, "A Time to Write," *Mississippi State Alumnus Magazine*, Winter 1990, http://lib.msstate.edu/grisham/timetowrite.php.

3. Henry Ford, quoted in Rob Brown, *Operation Breakthrough: Striving through Struggles for Success by Teaming* (Hoboken, NJ: John Wiley & Sons, 2016), 236.

4. H. G. Liddell, R. Scott, H. S. Jones, and R. McKenzie, *A Greek-English Lexicon* (Oxford: Clarendon Press, 1996), s.v. "timao."

Chapter 8 A New Kind of Awesome

1. "Driving Them Crazy: Americans' Top Customer Service Complaints," *Consumer Reports*, November 2, 2015, http://www.consumer

reports.org/cro/news/2015/11/top-customer-service-complaints/index
.htm.

2. Louw and Nida, eds., *Greek-English Lexicon of the New Testament*, s.v. "arete."

3. Kittel, Friedrich, and Bromiley, eds., *Theological Dictionary of the New Testament*, s.v. "arete."

4. Kittel, Friedrich, and Bromiley, eds., *Theological Dictionary of the New Testament*, s.v. "arete."

5. "Arete," Theoi Greek Mythology, July 2017, http://www.theoi.com /Daimon/Arete.html.

6. Betsy Morris, "Steve Jobs Speaks Out," *Fortune*, March 7, 2008, http://archive.fortune.com/galleries/2008/fortune/0803/gallery.jobsqna .fortune/4.html.

7. Kittel, Friedrich, and Bromiley, eds., *Theological Dictionary of the New Testament*, s.v. "arete."

8. C. S. Lewis, "First and Second Things," in *God in the Dock: Essays on Theology and Ethics* (Grand Rapids: Eerdmans, 1994), 280.

9. Martin Luther King Jr., "What Is Your Life's Blueprint," *Seattle Times*, October 26, 1967, http://old.seattletimes.com/special/mlk/king /words/blueprint.html.

Chapter 9 Your Ace in the Hole

1. H. R. Balz and G. Schneider, *Exegetical Dictionary of the New Testament* (Grand Rapids: Eerdmans, 1990), s.v. "epainos."

2. Liddell, Scott, Jones, and McKenzie, *A Greek-English Lexicon*, s.v. "epainos."

3. G. K. Chesterton, *St. Francis of Assisi* (New York: Image Books, 1957), 78.

Jamie Rasmussen (MDiv, Trinity Evangelical Divinity School) is the senior pastor of Scottsdale Bible Church, which has been regularly listed on *Outreach* magazine's Top 100 list in both size and speed of growth for the past ten years. He has been an ordained pastor for more than twenty-five years and has served growing churches in Detroit, Michigan; London, Ontario (Canada); and Cleveland, Ohio. He lives in Arizona.